LINGUISTIC SURVEYS OF AFRICA

Volume 10

BANTU

BANTU
Modern Grammatical, Phonetical, and Lexicographical Studies since 1860

CLEMENT M. DOKE

Routledge
Taylor & Francis Group
LONDON AND NEW YORK

First published in 1945 by Percy Lund, Humphries & Co. Ltd.

This edition first published in 2018
by Routledge
2 Park Square, Milton Park, Abingdon, Oxon OX14 4RN

and by Routledge
711 Third Avenue, New York, NY 10017

Routledge is an imprint of the Taylor & Francis Group, an informa business

© 1945 International African Institute

All rights reserved. No part of this book may be reprinted or reproduced or utilised in any form or by any electronic, mechanical, or other means, now known or hereafter invented, including photocopying and recording, or in any information storage or retrieval system, without permission in writing from the publishers.

Trademark notice: Product or corporate names may be trademarks or registered trademarks, and are used only for identification and explanation without intent to infringe.

British Library Cataloguing in Publication Data
A catalogue record for this book is available from the British Library

ISBN: 978-1-138-08975-4 (Set)
ISBN: 978-1-315-10381-5 (Set) (ebk)
ISBN: 978-1-138-09569-4 (Volume 10) (hbk)
ISBN: 978-1-138-09581-6 (Volume 10) (pbk)
ISBN: 978-1-315-10557-4 (Volume 10) (ebk)

Publisher's Note
The publisher has gone to great lengths to ensure the quality of this reprint but points out that some imperfections in the original copies may be apparent.

Disclaimer
The publisher has made every effort to trace copyright holders and would welcome correspondence from those they have been unable to trace.

BANTU

Modern Grammatical, Phonetical, and Lexicographical Studies since 1860

by

CLEMENT M. DOKE

Published for
INTERNATIONAL AFRICAN INSTITUTE
by
PERCY LUND, HUMPHRIES & CO. LTD.
12 Bedford Square, London, w.c.1

1945

PRINTED BY THE REPLIKA PROCESS
IN GREAT BRITAIN BY
LUND HUMPHRIES
LONDON · BRADFORD

FOREWORD

The International African Institute has received a grant from the Colonial Development and Welfare Fund to undertake preparatory work for a Handbook of African Languages. The need for a definitive and comprehensive survey and analysis of African Languages had long been recognised in the Institute, and work began in June, 1944.

The Handbook is being planned, with the aid of a committee of experts and a panel of consultants, to provide a systematic and critical study of the incidence, distribution and inter-relations of the different African Languages and dialects, as well as of the numbers speaking the several languages and dialects, and the extent of literacy among these different groups. It will also include critical bibliographies of publications relating to the various language groups, including grammars, dictionaries, and text-books, and a review of vernacular literature with special reference to its use for educational and other purposes.

In the initial stages the work will be largely concerned with the examination and assessment of material already available in print or manuscript. This will at the same time reveal needs for further information and for additional research in the field, to be carried out ad hoc or in collaboration with other Institutions and individuals in the different areas.

The present volume by Professor C.M. Doke is a preliminary survey of part of the field to be covered. It deals with literature on the Bantu languages and is being published in order to give all students who can assist in the survey, the benefit of the author's very extensive knowledge of the Bantu field. As he himself emphasises, this survey of Bantu studies is necessarily incomplete and the classification adopted is only tentative. The Institute considers, however, that such a preliminary study of this very wide and complex field will be of considerable value to all students of African languages; and it will have served a most useful purpose, if, as a result of its publication, gaps in existing knowledge are made more apparent, and further problems can be tackled more effectively. Those in possession of additional material, published or unpublished, will, it is hoped, be encouraged to make their information and hypotheses available as soon as possible. Both Professor Doke himself and the Linguistic Advisory Committee of the International African Institute will welcome comments, criticisms and additions which can be incorporated, with due acknowledgement, in later publications and will contribute to the Handbook in its final form.

Daryll Forde.
Director of the
International African
Institute

Ida Ward.
Chairman of the
Linguistic Advisory
Committee.

B A N T U
Modern Grammatical Phonetical and Lexicographical Studies since 1860

FOR the purpose of considering in some order the large amount and diverse nature of the contributions to our knowledge of Bantu languages in modern times, it is necessary to put forward some classification of the Bantu languages themselves. There is such a large number of languages of which some record or other has been made and the designations of the languages and dialects are so diverse and confusing that it is essential to attempt to sort them out and evolve some order out of the chaos. In this present study it is not our purpose to record all the dialects, or even all the languages, but to make reference only to the more important, to those in which some grammatical or other study has been done.

No final classification of Bantu languages has, as yet, been made. All we can advance at this stage is a tentative one, which may act as a basis for future correction and emendation. We divide Bantu languages, first of all into zones, areas characterised by uniform or similar linguistic phenomena. This is mainly a geographical classification. It must be realized that individual members of a particular zone may today be living among members of a different zone owing to tribal migrations (as is the case with the Ngoni, South-eastern zone, who are found among the Eastern Bantu), but the zone label is taken from the habitat of the majority. While languages belonging to one zone differ in certain essential phenomena from languages belonging to another zone, yet languages belonging to the same zone need not be mutually understood. Within the zones are groups, aggregations of languages possessing common salient phonetic and grammatical features, and having a high degree of mutual understanding, so that members can, without real difficulty, converse with one another. Naturally individual cases may arise (as with Kalanga or Western Shona, which cannot join the Shona unification) in which one section of the group has developed historically out of great mutual intelligibility with the other members, and yet must still be considered as belonging to that group. Again, within the groups are clusters, aggregations of dialects which contribute to, or use, a common literary form; and the possibility of the literary unification of the clusters belonging to the same group must not be lost sight of. Dialects are local vernaculars recognised by the Native speakers under special names. It is generally the case that there is a considerable number of dialects contributing to any given literary form in Bantu.[1]

---
[1] For these definitions see Doke: Bantu Linguistic Terminology.

Following is a tentative classification of the Bantu zones:

(1) North-western (Duala, Fang, etc.).
(2) Northern (Ganda, Rundi, etc.).
(3) Congo (Kongo, Bangi, etc.).
(4) Central (Luba, Bemba, etc.).
(5) Eastern (Shambala, Chaga, etc.), with which may be associated North-eastern (Swahili), and East-central (Nyanja).
(6) South-eastern (Nguni, Sotho, etc.), with which may be associated South-central (Shona).
(7) Western (Mbundu, Herero, etc.), with which may be associated West-central (Lwena).

It is obvious that the above classification is very general. Division into groups and clusters has only been worked out fully in the South-eastern zone, and at present we must content ourselves with picking out important members from the other zones. We shall now treat them in the order given.

[1] NORTH-WESTERN ZONE

Position: Languages of this zone abut upon the semi-Bantu and Sudanic languages of West Africa. They are to be found in the North-west corner of Bantu Africa, and are mostly distributed throughout the Cameroons and the Gabun district of French Equatorial Africa.

Characteristics: The main distinguishing features of the zone are:

(i) Monosyllabic prefix forms.
(ii) Moderate inflexion of the verb — inflexion not being so great as elsewhere in Bantu.
(iii) Noun prefix forms rather distinct from anywhere else in Bantu.
(iv) The use of a nasal consonant commonly to end a syllable.

There is distinct evidence that these languages have been influenced by semi-Bantu and Sudanic languages. They cannot be considered typical of Bantu linguistically, even as the people are not typical of Bantu physically.

The most important languages[1] in this zone are:

(a) Bube.
(b) Duala, Isubu, Nkosi, Basa, Lundu.
(c) Benga.
(d) Mpongwe.
(e) Fang, Yaunde and Bulu.
(f) Kele and Duma, with Ndumu.

---

[1] For detailed lists of the many languages and dialects recorded see H. H. Johnston's 'Comparative Study', Nos.183-226.

(a) Bube, the northern dialect of the language of Fernando Pô, referred to by Bleek, Torrend, Johnston and others as 'Fernandian' was early analysed by John Clarke.[1] Since 1860 little work of material importance has been done on this or other dialects of the Island. In 1881 was issued from the Primitive Methodist Mission Press Parr's Bubi na English Dictionary, with notes on grammar.[2] In 1887-8 Oskar Baumann published in the 'Z.A.S.' an article Beiträge zur Kenntniss der Bube-Sprache.[3] In 1890, however, appeared a very interesting book, the first and almost the only Bantu grammar written in Spanish; this is Father Joaquín Juanola's Primer Paso á la Lengua Bubí.[4] The first part of this book (up to page 88) deals with the northern dialect, the second part comprises mainly appendices dealing with the western dialect at San Carlos and the eastern dialect at Concepcion. Juanola's effort, though containing a certain amount of detailed information, is a model of what a Bantu grammar should not be. It would weary to give the many instances of this which one might quote. Let two suffice. In the first place he entirely missed the significance of the noun classes, calling the noun prefixes 'articles' as the Spanish el, la, lo, los and las. On page 20, for instance, he sets out four ways of forming plurals in Bube: (i) by adding a word of quantity, e.g. chobo > chobo nkenke; (ii) by inflexion, e.g. bompo > bempo; (iii) by inflexion and addition, e.g. eria > biria; and (iv) by change of word ('por cambio de Palabra'), lottó > mattó. In the second place, his verb classifications are hopelessly mixed; in one of these (page 61) he makes the division into auxiliary, regular, irregular, reflexive, reciprocal and impersonal, shewing no grasp of the principle of verbal derivatives.

As an effective Bantu language Bube, of course, will not find a place.

(b) Duala is spoken on the Cameroons mainland opposite the Island of Fernando Pô. Since the outstanding work of Saker in this language, and that of Merrick in its cognate Isubu in the fifties of last century, little[5] was done on Duala grammar until 1892 when Th.Christaller published his Handbuch der Dualasprache, which Meinhof considers a very considerable advance upon Saker's grammar. The first 68 pages are devoted to grammatical notes, followed by a text of folk-lore and some pages of phrases, while pages 91-214 comprise a 'Wörterbuch', Duala-Deutsch and

---

1 Bantu Language Pioneers of the Nineteenth Century, in 'B.St.', Vol.XIV, p.238. [Referred to in following pages as 'Bantu Pioneers'.]
2 Pp.xv, 40.
3 In this various dialectal vocabularies are given; pp.138-155.
4 Madrid, pp.189; note also Salvadó's work on Benga in 1891.
5 Meinhof published two short papers in the 'Z.A.S.',1888, and a Vocabulary (without author's name) was published from the 'Mission Press' (63pp.) in 1862.

Deutsch-Duala. Seidel also has some praise for Christaller's 'Handbuch', though he says that it is not without a number of mistakes and misconceptions, citing his lack of understanding of the 'relativpartikel'.[1] A. Seidel himself published, in the same year, his Leitfaden zur Erlernung der Duala-Sprache in Kamerun, a very slight grammatical treatise followed by vocabularies.[2] In 1904 he published, in the series of language manuals 'Methode Gaspey-Otto-Sauer', Die Duala-Sprache in Kamerun.[3] This comprises some 36 pages of grammatical notes, followed by about 80 pages of a systematic word-list with short phrases. For the scientific study of Duala however, we turn to the work of C. Meinhof. Chapter VII[4] of his Lautlehre der Bantusprachen published in 1899 (second edition 1910) contains a clear scientific exposition of the phonology of Duala, bringing it into line with his Ur-Bantu Studies. In 1912 Meinhof produced Die Sprache der Duala in Kamerun, Volume IV of Reimer's 'Deutsche Kolonialsprachen', a series of little language handbooks with exercises and vocabulary. There is nothing special to note regarding the grammatical work which is of the slightest in this little book.[5] An important contribution to our knowledge of Duala came with the production in 1914 of E. Dinkelacker's Wörterbuch der Duala-Sprache[6]. This is a carefully prepared vocabulary[7], Duala-German and German-Duala, in which all the tones of the entries have been marked. Seidel had given some slight attention to tone in his later work, but here tone-marking is used consistently. The whole problem of tone in Duala is discussed at length and in a masterly way by H.J. Melzian in his article Die Frage der Mitteltöne im Duala in the 'M.S.O.S.', Vol.XXXIII (pp.159-212) in 1930. P.H. Nekes had previously, in 1911, contributed a short article entitled Die Musikalischen Töne in der Duala-sprache to 'Ant.' (Vol.VI, pp.911-919). In 1910 the missionary Bufe contributed to the 'Z.f.K.S.' (Vol.I, pp.25-36) a lexical comparison of Duala with four neighbouring dialects, entitled Die Dualasprache in ihrem Verhältnis zu den Dialekten des Nordgebiets der Station Bombe. In 1928 E.A.L. Gaskin published a little Outline Duala Grammar. The most scholarly treatment of Duala grammar appeared in 1939. This was Johannes Ittmann's Grammatik des Duala[8], in the preparation of which he acknowledged the assistance of Carl Meinhof. In this important work the first 34 pages are devoted to a detailed study of the phonology including tone analysis. Both this and the grammatical part which follows are built up on the scheme of Professor Meinhof for Ur-Bantu, and the whole is rich in examples. Especially valuable are Ittmann's two large sections on Word-formation (36 pages) and Syntax (72 pages), in the latter of which the laws of sentence struc-

---

1 A. Seidel, Die Duala-Sprache in Kamerun, page iii.
2 pp.ix + 83; a reprint of this appeared in 1912.
3 'Systematisches Wörterverzeichnis und Einführung in die Grammatik', pp.viii + 119.
4 pp. 92-109 (pp.142-170 of the 2nd edition).
5 pp. xv + 119. On pp.v & vi is a short list of Duala books, though strangely enough Meinhof does not mention any of Seidel's works.
6 'A.Hamb.K.I.', XVI, pp.215.
7 Containing over 5000 Duala words.
8 Supplement to the 'Z.f.K.S.', No.20; pp.250.

ture in Duala are minutely expounded and fully illustrated. L. Reallon, Administrateur des Colonies, produced Premiers éléments de langage Douala.[1]

For Isubu, the only modern work to be noted is Meinhof's Das Verbum in der Isubu-Sprache, contributed to the 'Z.A.S.',[2] 1889–1890. In the allied Kwiri, E.Schuler contributed to the 'M.S.O.S.'[3] in 1908 Die Sprache der Bakwiri, and C.H. Swarg wrote a 'Vocabulary'.

Nkosi, of West Cameroons, is described by H. Dorsch as a distorted dialect of Duala. The Sudanic influence in its phonology has prompted some to deny its being a Bantu language, but this is not the case. Dorsch provided in 1911 an interesting grammatical outline in his Grammatik der Nkosi-Sprache mit einer des Nkosi mit Duala vergleichenden Einteitung in the 'Z.f.K.S.'[4]; and followed this by a useful Vocabularium der Nkosi-Sprache in following numbers of the same journal.[5]

Basa, spoken to the south and east of Duala, though having affinities therewith, is also heavily influenced phonologically by Sudanic. The first analysis of this language is that by S.Rosenhuber, Die Basá-Sprache, in the 'M.S.O.S.' Vol.XI, pp.219–306. This contribution, published in 1908, contains a short grammatical sketch, followed by vocabularies of 'Deutsch-Basá' and 'Basá-Deutsch'. In 1912 was published posthumously at Hamburg Georg Schürle's Die Sprache der Basa in Kamerun[6] edited by Carl Meinhof. This work consisted of a grammatical study (pp.1–86) followed by Basa-Deutsch and Deutsch-Basa vocabularies occupying pages 89 to 292, a very considerable study. H. Skolaster contributed in 1914 an article to 'Ant.' (Vol.IX. pp.740–759) on Die Musikalischen Töne in der Basa-Sprache. In this comparisons were made with the Koko and Yaunde languages. A Basa-French Beginners' Book has also been published by the Presbyterian Mission.

Lundu: A.Bruens produced in 1937 a little cyclostyled Grammar of Lundu (of 51 pp.quarto); the language, claimed to be the most north-westerly Bantu language, is allied to Duala but much influenced by Sudanic Efik.

(c) Benga is spoken some distance south of the Duala area on the southward coast of Spanish Guinea (Rio Muni). In 1892 R.H. Nassau published a revised edition of Mackey's grammar[7], and in 1889–90 Meinhof published

---
1 I have not seen this, and have no record of the date.
2 Jahrg. 3, pp.206–234.
3 Jahrg. XI, pp.174–218.
4 Vol.I, pp.241–283.
5 Vol.II, pp.161–193, 324–330 and Vol.III, pp.34–62; in the years 1911 and 1912.
6 Band VIII of the 'A.Hamb.K.I.'.
7 First published in 1855, cf.'Bantu Pioneers', p.241.

in the 'Z.A.S.'[1] a Discussion of the Benga Verb. In the previous volume[2] he had made a short comparison between Benga and Duala. In 1891 F.Salvadó y Cos published at Madrid Collección de apuntes preliminares sobre la lengua Benga, etc.[3]

(d) Mpongwe is spoken in the Gabun area of French Equatorial Africa, the purest dialect being found around Libreville on the Gabun Estuary, though dialectal forms, including that of Galwa, extend southward below Cape Lopez and along the Ogowe River. A second edition of J.L. Wilson's pioneer work on Mpongwe Grammar[4] was published in New York in 1879; in which same year were published Heads of Mpongwe Grammar — 'containing most of the principles needed by a learner. By a late missionary.Gaboon, West Africa' (pp.59), and A Vocabulary of the Mpongwe language,' by American missionaries, at Gaboon, West Africa' (pp.6-54)[5]. Apart from this we are practically entirely indebted to French Catholic missionaries of the Gabun for work in this language. There is an undated, unauthenticated Essai sur la grammaire npongue, which is supplemented by 'dictionnaires' 'français-npongue' and 'npongue-français' (pp.38, 52, 48). Father Le Berre published his Grammaire de la Language Pongouée[6] in 1873. In this is a great amount of information, classified unfortunately on non-Bantu principles. Le Berre does not attempt to regularise or explain the remarkable sound-changes occurring in the verb conjugation and under nasal influence in certain noun classes; in fact he records but four noun classes, noting as 'exceptions' several forms which represent other classes. In 1912 Father J.M.Gautier of the Catholic Mission at Libreville published a vastly superior treatise, Grammaire de la Langue Mpongwée[7], in which he made a classification of seven noun classes (singular and plural together), and tackled the problem of the 'strong' and 'weak' initials in varying parts of the verb conjugation.[8] His book is an extremely good piece of work including a treatment of syntax and much up-to-date handling. The question of word-division needs yet to be faced, and a correction in classification of certain parts of speech, particularly pronouns and prepositions.

Missionaries of the 'Congrégation du Saint-Esprit et du Saint Coeur de Marie' in the Gabun produced two most serviceable dictionaries, Dictionnaire Français-Pongoué[9] in 1877, and Dictionnaire Pongoué-

---

1 Vol.3, pp.265-284.
2 Vol.2, pp.190-208 (1888/89).
3 pp.151; I have not seen a copy of this.
4 In 1847; see 'Bantu Pioneers', p.239.
5 I have not seen these, probably they are but re-statements of Wilson's work.
6 pp.223.
7 pp.xv + 250.
8 Cf. pp. 81, 82, also p.9.
9 354 pp., double column.

Français[1] in 1881. Fathers Le Berre and Delorme had part in these works. Both books are enriched by idiomatic examples illustrating the use of the words. The second dictionary is preceded by a disquisition on the principles of the language, occupying pages xi-xxxix; this is but a condensation of Le Berre's Grammar and adds nothing new. A very large[2] Dictionnaire Mpongue-Français was published by A. Walker in 1934; I have not seen a copy of this.

Omyene or Galwa, a dialect of Mpongwe, was illustrated in 1908 by M. Robert's Méthode pour l'étude de l'Omyene, including grammar and vocabulary.

(e) Fang, or as the French call it 'Pahouin', is spoken by a fairly numerous people inhabiting Spanish Guinea and the Gabun area of French Equatorial Africa as far south as the Central Ogowe. The people were reputed to be inveterate cannibals. There are several dialects of Fang, the most important of which is Makei, and closely allied to this language are Yaunde and Bulu. One of the earliest publications on Fang was a Fañwe Primer and Vocabulary[3] compiled by H.M.Adams of the Gaboon Mission (A.B.C.F.M.) who died in 1856; the manuscript was revised in 1878 by J. Bushnell and published by R.H. Nassau in 1881. In 1887 R.N. Cust published, at his own charges, A.O. Zabala's Diccionario Pámue-Español with the title-page reading 'Vocabulary of the Fan Language'.[4] Señor Zabala was an explorer on behalf of the Spanish Government. A notable work was that published by Father L. Lejeune in 1892, Dictionnaire Français-Fang, which treated of the Makei dialect of Ogowe. The 'dictionary' comprised 295 pages double-column of vocabulary preceded by a grammatical outline — quelques principes grammaticaux — of 51 pages. This grammatical outline was reprinted two years later[5] in Volume XXIV of the 'Actes de la Société Philologique'. A Fang-Français Vocabulary did not appear until well into the 20th Century, when L. Martrou, Vicar Apostolic of the Gabun, produced his Lexique Fãñ-Français. In this little book of 137 pages (vocabulary double column of 117 pp., preceded by a grammatical outline) the author uses a new orthography based on the principles of Ch. Sacleux's 'Essai de Phonétique'.[6] The book is a useful companion to that of Lejeune. In 1901, however, had appeared V. Largeau's great Encyclopédie Pahouine. This is really a cyclopaedic dictionary 'Français-Fang'; first there is a general introduction of some 70 pages covering a description of the people and grammatical notes; this is followed by over 600 pages of detailed work on the French words included. Some single

---

1 pp.xxxix + 287, double column.
2 pp.640, xvii.
3 pp.199; 'Phrases' pp.1-97, Vocabulary, Fang-English, pp.99-199.
4 S.P.C.K. London, pp.viii+ 34.
5 The reprint (corresponding page for page) bears the date 1894, but represents 'Année 1895' of the 'Actes'.
6 This is the only clue to the date, for Sacleux's work appeared in 1905.

entries occupy several pages, as for instance 'palabre' — legal process — which takes twelve pages including numerous Fang texts with translation. It might be criticised — as may also van der Burgt's greater work on Rundi — that such a work should be based on the Fang words and not the French. Nevertheless Largeau has done a great service to the Fang language by this comprehensive publication.

Yaunde, spoken in the hinterland of west Cameroons, is closely allied to the Fang language. It was first brought to notice by a brief vocabulary in Meinhof's Die Sprachverhältnisse in Kamerun[1] in 1895. The first grammatical description was given by Father M. Haarpaintner in 1909 in his Grammatik der Yaundesprache which was published in two parts in 'Ant'.[2] This is but a brief outline of 28 pages. On the grammatical side the man who has made the greatest contribution in Yaunde is Father H. Nekes who published in 1911 in the series 'Lehrb.S.O.S.(Berlin)' (Band XXVI) his Lehrbuch der Jaunde-Sprache. This very comprehensive study of the language gives adequate attention to the phonology and tonology of Yaunde. The 207 pages of grammar are divided into (i) Lautlehre, (ii) Tonlehre, (iii) Wortbildungslehre, and (iv) Formenlehre, which last section of 160 pages of formal grammatical study is divided into 56 lessons with a large number of exercises. To this are added two appendices in which Nekes is associated with W.Planert; these comprise exercises dealing particularly with tone,[3] and a 'Jaunde-Deutsch' and 'Deutsch-Jaunde' Wörterbuch. The whole work impresses one with its thoroughness, especially the thorough way in which the question of tone has been handled, and the employment of five symbols for tone-marking. Two years later, in 1913, Nekes wrote Die Sprache der Jaunde in Kamerun[4], a more concise study, as Volume V of the series 'Deutsche Kolonialsprachen'. Another worker who has contributed largely to our knowledge of Yaunde is M. Heepe, who published in 1919 as Volume XXIV of the 'A.Hamb.K.I.' his Jaunde-Texte[5]. This large collection of textual material is accompanied by valuable phonological and grammatical information. Pages 1-19 are taken up by an experimental study in Yaunde tone. Then follow some 30 pages of phrases, while Section III comprises 90 pages of textual material supplied by Karl Atangana. Section IV gives some 45 pages of grammatical notes; while Section V, the rest of the book, is devoted to further textual material supplied by P. Messi. In 1926 Dr. Heepe published his Jaunde-Wörterbuch[6] in association with Father Nekes. This is a scholarly piece of work, a 'Jaunde-Deutsch' dictionary of 187 pages followed by a 'Deutsch-Jaunde' vocabulary.

---

1 In the 'Z.A.O.S.'
2 Vol.IV, pp.684-701, 919-930.
3 Nekes later contributed to the 'Festschrift P.W. Schmidt', in 1928. an important article Zur Tonologie in den Bantu-Sprachen (pp.80-92.)
4 pp.111.
5 pp.xvi + 325.
6 Published by the University of Hamburg, pp.xiv+257, double column.

One type of Yaunde is treated by Mgr. Graffin and R.P. Pichon in their Grammaire Ewondo.

The allied dialect of Bulu, of South-western Cameroons was first represented by G.T. v. Hagen's Lehrbuch der Bulu Sprache in 1914. This contains three parts. Part I consists of a short outline of grammar (pp.9-77) followed by brief treatments of Drum-language (Trommelsprache) and Songs with music. Part II, of Exercises (pp.87-202) contains, among other material for reading and translation, a number of folk tales. Part III is the vocabulary, 'Bulu-Deutsch' (pp.207-315) and 'Deutsch-Bulu' (pp.316-402). A much slighter work was Ch. Mathieu's Petit Vocabulaire Français-Boulou of 1921. This little vocabulary contains about 1500 entries arranged according to subject headings. G.L. Bates published in 1926 a Handbook with Bulu-English Vocabulary[1], and the Presbyterian Mission issued a Bulu-French Beginners' Book[2], with language notes. In 1932 R.A. Good produced his English-Bulu Vocabulary.

(f) Kele, (i.e. diKele to distinguish it from the Congo loKele)is spoken south of the Ogowe River, over a long but narrow area of South Gabun. Since the 1854 Grammar of Preston and Best[3], only sundry short collections of words have been published in this language. In the closely allied language of Duma, spoken on the upper Ogowe, there is A. Reeb's Essai de Grammaire Douma, a short outline of 48 pages published in 1895. In the same year Père Dahin produced his Vocabulaire Aduma-Français and Vocabulaire Français-Aduma.[4] Akin also is Ndumu, of which A. Biton published in 1907 his Dictionnaire Français-Ndumu et Ndumu Français[5], preceded by an outline of grammatical elements.

[2] NORTHERN ZONE

Position: The languages of this zone[6] are found in parts of Kenya Colony, Uganda and the area of Ruanda-Urundi of the Belgian Congo. Though this does not cover a very large area, it is the most densely populated part of Bantu Africa.

Characteristics: The main distinguishing features of this zone are:
(i) Disyllabic noun prefixes are general (except Kamba and Gikuyu), shown in their fullest form in the archaic Gishu, where each of the two syllables of the noun prefix has a consonant.

---
1 Halsey Memorial Press, pp.176. I have not seen this.
2 I have not seen these.
3 Cf. 'Bantu Pioneers', p.239.
4 I have not seen copies of these; pp.72 each.
5 Grammar pp.i-xxxii; Français-Ndumu, pp.178; Ndumu-Français, pp.97.
6 So called because of Roscoe's pioneer work on the area, entitled 'The Northern Bantu'.

(ii) Full prefixal type of locative formation, with the prefix e- as well as the prefixes of the three locative noun classes.
(iii) Wealth of augmentative prefixal formations for nouns.
(iv) The operation of Dahl's law of phonetic dissimilation.
(v) The use of interdental consonants, ө and ð in some languages; and double consonants in others.

There is evidence, particularly in Kamba and Gikuyu, that some of these languages have been influenced by Hamitic.

The most important languages in this zone are:

(a) Gishu.
(b) Konjo.
(c) Nyoro, with dialectal forms: Nkole, Toro, Kerewe, Karagwe, Ziba and Haya.
(d) Ganda, with Soga.
(e) Rundi, with Rwanda and Ha.
(f) Gikuyu.
(g) Kamba.

(a) <u>Gishu</u>, spoken by a small group north-west of Lake Victoria, also called 'Gisu' and 'Masaba' is considered to be the most archaic type of Bantu extant. Apart from slight vocabularies only one study has been made upon this language, viz. J.B. Purvis' <u>A Manual of Lumasala Grammar</u>, which was published by the S.P.C.K. in 1907. This is a valuable little exposition of 96 pages. In his introduction the author writes: 'There seems little doubt but that in the country of Masaba, i.e. the land on and near Mount Elgon, we have the most primitive language of what might well be called the Victoria Nyanza Bantu group'. The language is noted for its consonantal-commencing disyllabic noun prefixes, e.g. <u>babandu</u>, <u>kikindu</u>, <u>bibindu</u>, <u>kamabali</u>, etc.

(b) <u>Konjo</u>, bordering on the Semliki River and the great Congo forest land, is represented, apart from Gospel translation, only by some incidental short vocabularies collected by Johnston and Struck.

(c) <u>Nyoro</u>, of western Uganda, has only been illustrated by travellers' vocabularies and translations, apart from two works. The first is <u>An Elementary Lunyoro Grammar</u> by H.E. Maddox in 1902. This little work of 81 pages of grammar, followed by 77 pages of Nyoro-English and English-Nyoro vocabularies, deals with the western or <u>Toro</u> dialect of Nyoro. The second is <u>A Lunyoro-Lunyankole-English and English-Lunyoro-Lunyankole Dictionary</u>, by M.B. Davis, published in 1938[1]. The language is closely allied to that of Ganda. Considerable research work has been done on Nyoro by R.A. Snoxall, but it is still unpublished.

<u>Kerewe</u>, spoken on the large island of Bukerebe and the adjacent

---

1 Pp.332. I have not seen a copy of this.

peninsula and islands of Southern Victoria Nyanza, is illustrated by E. Hurel's contribution to the 'M.S.O.S' in 1909, entitled La Langue Kikerewe.[1] This contains an outline exposition of the grammar, with special attention to syntax. Old methods are followed, including the recording of 'prepositions'. Several pages are devoted to folk-tales in Kerewe text and interlinear French translation. This is followed by some thirty pages of Kerewe-French vocabulary, double column.

The Ziba dialect, of the south and south-west coasts of Lake Victoria, was well described by H. Rehse in his Die Sprache der Baziba in Deutsch-Ostafrika, which appeared in three parts in the 'Z.f.K.S.', 1912-13 (Vol. III, pp.1-33, 81-123 and 201-229). In this, pronunciation, grammar and syntax are given and exercises provided. Rehse used a modified form of conjunctive writing. Captain Herrmann had previously, in 1904, contributed a useful study of this language to the 'M.S.O.S.'[2], entitled Lusíba, die Sprache der Länder Kisíba, Bugábu, Kjamtwára, Kjánja und Ihángiro.

(d) Ganda is the most important of the Northern Bantu languages. It is spoken in a great part of Uganda, especially from the north-western and northern shores of Lake Victoria, and is recognised as an official language in the Protectorate. Apart from a brief vocabulary recorded by H.M. Stanley[3], the first linguistic study of Ganda which we have was the Outline Grammar of the Lu-ganda Language published in 1882 by C.T. Wilson of the C.M.S.[4] Several of the White Fathers in Uganda devoted their attention to the language and of them L. Livinhac was the pioneer. In 1884 he sent to headquarters in Algeria (not for publication) an Essai de Grammaire Ruganda[5]; this was published the following year, but a French-Ganda dictionary which he carried with him the following year was lost — original and copy — in the wreck of 'l'Immaculée-Conception'. Livinhac later revised his work, to which were added contributions by C. Denoit, and after the latter's death, a second edition, entitled Manuel de Langue Luganda[6], was published in 1894. In addition to a straightforward description of the grammar and syntax this contained 130 pages of legends and fables with interlinear French translation. A third edition, enlarged into a veritable 'tome' of nearly 500 large pages[7] appeared in 1914 under the editorship of Father Le Veux. This is a most valuable contribution to the idiomatic study of Ganda and contains an enormous amount of illustrative material. A new edition of more concise grammatical detail, entitled Grammaire Luganda[8], was edited by A. Wolters in 1921, and contained

---

1 Vol.12, pp.1-113.
2 Vol.VII, pp.150-200.
3 In Through the Dark Continent, p.486, in 1878.
4 I have not seen a copy of this; pp.xii, 158.
5 pp.xiii + 98.
6 pp.290.
7 pp.xv + 475
8 pp.xiii + 238.

a foreword by Leon Livinhac, Bishop of Pacando. Meanwhile G.L.Pilkington, of the Church Missionary Society, produced a remarkably fine little Handbook of Luganda in 1891[1]. In this the grammatical elements are set out in a clear, concise and handy way; reprints appeared in 1901, 1911 and 1917. Pilkington also published, in 1892, a Luganda-English and English-Luganda Vocabulary[2], containing a useful collection of words, and some practical appendices, the third of which was a comparison of Swahili and Ganda. The untimely death of Pilkington[3] in the Sudanese mutiny in 1897 deprived Ganda studies of one full of great promise. W. A. Crabtree of the C.M.S., working upon Pilkington's 'Hand-book' and copious additional notes and translations of his, produced in 1902 Elements of Luganda Grammar[4], with which he included exercises and a vocabulary. This latter inclusion was from Pilkington's collection. Crabtree brought his work more up to date in A Manual of Lu-ganda[5], which was published at Cambridge in 1921. In this he paid considerable attention to phonetics, and though there are many things one may criticise in his work, Crabtree's manual has proved of great value. It is unfortunate that Crabtree's flair for phonetics led him into the supra-speculative atmosphere in which he published his two volumes of Primitive Speech (Part I, 'A Study in African Phonetics', S.P.C.K. 1922; and Part II, 'The Prefix System of Bantu', Kegan Paul, 1922). In these he drew largely upon his store of material in Ganda and allied languages. Later, Crabtree devoted his time mainly to researches into Sumerian in his obsession that that language was the precursor of Bantu.

Lexicographical work in Ganda was represented first by Pilkington's vocabulary of 1892, already referred to; then in 1902 by H.H. Johnston's brief vocabulary in his 'Uganda Protectorate'[6]. In 1904 appeared G.R. Blackledge's Luganda-English and English-Luganda Vocabulary[7]. About the same time, but undated, was published the fragmentary Collections of a Lexicon in Lu-ganda and English, etc.[8] by P. O'Flaherty. P.H. Le Veux brought out in 1917 his Premier Essai de Vocabulaire Luganda-Français d'après l'ordre étymologique[9], a very modest title for a very considerable Ganda dictionary, in which he concentrated on the etymological, while not overlooking the idiomatic. Father Le Veux's dictionary may be reckoned among the dozen or so really important Bantu dictionaries; and we may consider that Le Veux has contributed more than anyone else to exact knowledge of the Ganda Language.

1 pp.vi + 95, S.P.C.K.
2 pp.211.
3 Cf. Pilkington of Uganda by C.F. Harford-Battersby.
4 pp.266.
5 pp.xx + 254.
6 pp.897-8, also including a language study on pp.980 et seq.
7 S.P.C.K. Later edition 1921, pp.211, double column.
8 I have not seen a copy of this; [1892] pp.41.
9 Maison-Carrée, pp.1047, single col.

Two other Ganda studies need mention here: C.W. Hattersley and H.W. Duta produced in 1904[1] their Luganda Phrases and Idioms; while Canon F. Rowling contributed in 1912 his Guide to Luganda Prose Composition[2], which is remarkable in that it is almost the only book yet produced aiming at a study of composition, as a subject, in any Bantu language. It is a very useful book — its aim being to help students and candidates for language examinations.

In 1906 J. Gorju published his Essai de grammaire comparée: du Ruganda au Runyoro et au Runyankole.[3]

(e) Rundi and Rwanda are closely allied languages though treated as two literary forms. They are spoken by a very large population in the Ruanda-Urundi province of the Congo Belge to the South-west of Lake Victoria.

The best-known name in connection with Rundi is that of J.M.M. van der Burgt who wrote first his Eléments d'une grammaire Kirundi, which appeared in the 'M.S.O.S.'[4], in 1902, and followed this, the next year, with his monumental Dictionnaire Français-Kirundi[5]. This remarkable work is a mine of cyclopaedic information, containing interspersed 196 ethnographic articles concerning the country and the people. There is a long general introduction dealing with African history and foreign influence upon Africa, to a certain degree speculative, with such questionable digressions as that upon 'Atlantis'. The dictionary itself, based on the French words (it is a pity it is not Rundi-Français instead), is extremely well done, containing, apart from cyclopaedic material, a vast collection of idioms and illustrative sentences. The value of the work was further enhanced (for the area was at that time under German administration) by including, in each case, the Swahili and German equivalent bracketed after the French entry. A long supplement is added dealing with 'Imana' the concept of the deity, and other religious beliefs, with additional notes on the history of certain of the tribes. In 1908 F. Ménard began his contributions to Rundi by the publication of his Grammaire Rundi[6], a straightforward description of the language of considerable practical use to learners. Quite a third of this book is rightly devoted to the study of syntax. It is a valuable contribution. In 1909 Ménard produced his Dictionnaire Français-Kirundi et Kirundi-Français[7], a handy concise book of reference, designed for practical use rather than any exhaustive treatment; while in the following year appeared his Guide de Conversation Kirundi[8], a very ex-

---

1 Second ed. 1921, S.P.C.K. pp.128.
2 2nd edition 1921, S.P.C.K., pp.147.
3 pp.vi, 42.
4 Band V, pp.1-78; with a supplement (pp.79-108) on the language of the Pygmies.
5 Bois-le-duc, Holland, 1903; pp. cxix + 640, double col. with numerous illustrations and a map.
6 Maison-Carrée, Algeria, 1908; pp.xiii + 516.
7 Published in Belgium, pp.xxvi + 262 + 308, with added blank leaves.
8 Maison-Carrée, Algeria, 1910; pp.507.

haustive phrase and conversation book. All these works are thoroughly reliable.

For Rwanda we are mainly indebted to E. Hurel, who contributed to the 'M.S.O.S.' in 1911 his Manuel Rwanda.[1] This appeared in book form as a second edition, under the title Grammaire Kinyarwanda, the third edition[2] appearing in 1931. Certain exercises were included in this little book. In 1913 appeared Father Dufay's Deutsch-Kinjaruanda-Wörterbuch. In 1917 K. Roehl contributed Das Dahlsche Gesetz und verwandte Erscheinungen im Ruanda-Rundi-Ha to the 'Z.f.K.S.'[3], in which paper he discussed the incidence of Dahl's Law of dissimilation in this group of languages. In 1926 Hurel published a Dictionnaire français-Runyarwanda et Runyarwanda-français[4] During the years 1921-1931 P. Schumacher contributed to 'Ant.' certain papers entitled La Phonétique du Kinyarwanda in which a good deal of grammatical material was included. Nothing of any importance has been done upon Ha.

(f) Gikuyu[5], commonly referred to as 'Kikuyu', is spoken in the highlands of Kenya Colony between the Upper Tana and the Meru and Nyeri districts on the northern slopes of Mt. Kenya; south-west to the vicinity of Nairobi; and eastwards to the Teraka country. There are several dialects of Gikuyu. The first monograph on this language was A. Hemery's English-Kikuyu Handbook[6] containing a simple grammatical outline, an English-Kikuyu vocabulary and a few pages of phrases. In 1904 A.W. McGregor published his English-Kikuyu Vocabulary[7], a handy little book; and in the following year A Grammar of the Kikuyu Language[8], in which the essentials are recorded with the usual European bias of the time and often inappropriate terminology; the nasal changes are well recorded. In 1914 appeared A.R. Barlow's Tentative Studies in Kikuyu Grammar and Idiom.[9] This well-presented publication is divided into two parts, the first (pp. 9-77) deals with graded studies and exercises for beginners, while the second (pp.78-197) deals with more formal grammar, a considerable advancement being shown on the method previously followed by McGregor. This is a valuable book for the student of Gikuyu. Barlow mentions two further works on the language, which I have not yet seen, viz: J.E.Henderson's Easy Gikuyu Lessons, and an Italian-Kikuyu and Kikuyu-Italian Dictionary, published by the Italian Mission in British East Africa. The Catholic Mission at Nyeri

---

1 pp.1-159
2 Maison-Carrée, Algeria; pp.265.
3 Vol.8, pp.197-207.
4 I have not seen a copy of this.
5 By Dahl's law of dissimilation 'k' in a syllable before another 'k' becomes 'ɣ' (voiced).
6 pp.87; 14 pages of grammar, 60 pages of vocab.
7 S.P.C.K. pp.192.
8 S.P.C.K. 1905, pp.160.
9 pp.236.

published in 1931 a <u>Lexicon Latinum-Kikuyense</u> of 326 pages (double col.) and a <u>Lexicon Kikuyense-Latinum</u> of 73 pages. In 1940 appeared the late Miss L. Armstrong's monumental <u>Phonetic and Tonal Structure of Kikuyu</u>[1], a model of meticulous investigation and recording. This is the first book in which tonal grammar has been properly worked out for any Bantu language, and should serve as a model for similar work in other Bantu languages. It was published posthumously. L.J. and G.S.B. Beecher published, undated, <u>A Kikuyu-English Dictionary</u> in three volumes.

(g) <u>Kamba</u> is spoken between the Tana River in the north and Kilimanjaro on the south, being bounded on the west by Gikuyu and on the east by the Galla, Pokomo and Giriama tribes. Quite a number of vocabularies of Kamba appeared in various publications, by L. Krapf in his 'Vocabularies of Six East African Languages' in 1850, by A.D. Shaw in his 'Pocket Vocabulary of East African Languages' in 1885, by J.T. Last in his 'Polyglotta Africana Orientalis' in 1885, by C.G. Büttner[2] in 1888, by S. Watt[3] in 1900, by J. Hofmann[4] in 1901, and by H.R. Tate in the 'Journal of the Anthropological Institute' in June 1904. Apart from these, Last wrote a little <u>Grammar of the Kamba Language</u>[5] in 1885, and (Mrs.) H. Hinde, the author of 'A Masai Grammar', published in 1904 <u>Vocabularies of the Kamba and Kikuyu Languages of East Africa</u>[6], in which she dealt with two distinct Kamba dialects.[7] But the most important contribution to the study of this language is E. Brutzer's <u>Handbuch der Kambasprache</u>, which was contributed in 1906 to the 'M.S.O.S.'[8]. This is a full and detailed exposition of the grammatical elements of the language, though with rather a non-Bantu classification of the parts of speech. It contains considerable vocabulary and some textual material. In 1926 G. Lindblom published <u>Notes on Kamba Grammar</u>[9] which he indicated was meant to form a supplement to Brutzer's 'Handbuch'. Useful information is given upon the dialects and valuable phonological notes. The orthography is that used by Professor Lundell for Swedish dialect work. The most recent publication is a tentative roneod <u>Kikamba-English Dictionary</u> compiled by the Language Committee of the Africa Inland Mission in Ukamba, 1939. This foolscap typescript of 231 pages contains between 5000 and 6000 entries with considerable idiomatic detail.

---

1 Oxford University Press, pp.xviii + 363.
2 <u>Deutsch-Kikamba Wörterbuch</u>, pp.81-123, in the 'Z.f.A.S.'
3 <u>Vocabulary of the Kikamba language</u>, published by Kelker, Pennsylvania, U.S.A.
4 <u>Wörterbuch der Kambasprache, Kamba-deutsch</u> (limited number hectographed for the Leipziger Mission).
5 S.P.C.K. pp.40.
6 Cambridge, pp.xvii + 75.
7 A criticism of this very faulty work is given by Lindblom in his 'Notes', page 8, as well as an appraisement of several of the other publications.
8 Vol.IX, pp.1-100.
9 Vol.10 of the 'Archives d'études orientales', Uppsala, pp.1-100.

[3] CONGO ZONE

Position: The languages of this zone are found in the basin of the Central and Lower Congo River, covering large portions of Belgian Congo, part of Northern Angola and Southern French Congo. Details concerning this area may be found in Maes and Boone, *Les Peuplades du Congo Belge* and in W.H. Stapleton's *Comparative Handbook of Congo Languages*.

Characteristics: The main distinguishing features of this zone are:

(i) The occurrence of mostly monosyllabic prefix forms.
(ii) Vowel harmony, especially in verbal derivative forms; and verb terminal vowel commonly the same as the stem vowel; a strong vowel assimilation revealing itself.
(iii) Nasal assimilation in verbal derivative forms.
(iv) Verb infinitive commonly without prefix.
(v) A high development of verbal derivatives, with unusual compounding of suffixes.
(vi) Generally complicated tone system.

The most important languages[1] in this zone are:

(1) Kongo[2], with its two main branches:

    (a) kishiKongo and kiKongo.
    (b) kaKongo, with dialects, Yombe, Vili.

---

[1] J. Tanghe in an article contributed to 'Congo' in 1930, dealing with 'Lingala', places the languages 'used' in this area in the following order of importance:
    (1) Bangi and Ngala.
    (2) Kongo, Swahili, Ngombe and Lolo.
    (3) Poto, Soko and Kele.

[2] Laman divides Kongo according to eleven dialectal forms, as follows:

1 Central, Mazinga (spoken at Mukimbungu on both sides of the Congo river in the central part of Belgian Lower Congo); i.e. kiKongo.
2 Southern, San Salvador (spoken in Portuguese and adjoining Belgian territory); i.e. kishiKongo.
3 Eastern, dialect of Kisantu (spoken in eastern part of Belgian Lower Congo); kiKongo.
4 North-eastern, dialect of Madzia (spoken in French Lower Congo, west of Brazzaville).
5 Northern, dialect of Kingoyi or Bwende (spoken near middle of border between Belgian and French Congo.)
6 Bembe (spoken at Muyonzi in French Congo.)
7 North-western, Kunyi dialect of Ludima (spoken in French Congo).
8 Vili dialect of Loango (coastal area of French Congo).
9 Western or Kiyombe dialect (spoken in North-western part of Mayombe in Belgian Congo).
10 Mboka dialect of Kabinda, Angola.
11 Ndingi or Ndinzi dialect (spoken on border of Belgian Congo and Angola.

[Cf. Meinhof, *Bantu-Phonology*, pp.155-6].

(2) Ndongo [kiMbundu]

(3) North-eastern Congo:
    (a) Kele (loKele).
    (b) So.

(4) Middle Congo:
    (a) Poto.
    (b) Ngombe.
    (c) Mongo (Western dials. include Sengele, Bolia, Ntomba-nzale; Central dials. include Nkundu, Kela; Eastern dials. include Kuba, Tetela).
    (d) Ngala, with dials. Mabale, etc.
    (e) Bangi.

(5) Teke, with dialects, Ifumu, Tio.

(6) Bira.

(7) Bua.

This is only a very tentative classification, and it is possible that many of these languages, particularly of the Middle Congo, belong to groups quite distinct from one another.

(1) Kongo: This important language group is spoken in the vicinity of the mouth of the Congo River, its various types being found on either side of the river for a considerable distance, in the Belgian Congo, the French Congo and Angola. The early work of the Roman Catholic fathers, principally Brusciotto, has already been noticed[1]. Of modern workers the two most important names are those of Bentley and Laman. In connection with Kongo the localised term 'Fiote' is often used, more particularly in connection with the northern kaKongo type, and the careless 'commercial dialect'.[2]

(1a) kiKongo, spoken on the south bank of the Congo River towards its mouth, is here used to include the kishiKongo of San Salvador. S. Koelle's Polyglotta Africana, published in 1854, illustrated several vocabularies of this and the kaKongo clusters, kishiKongo being represented by 'Mimboma' and kiKongo to the eastward by 'Musentandu'. In 1882 H. Grattan Guiness, Director of the Livingstone (Congo) Inland Mission, published his Grammar of the Congo Language 'as spoken in the cataract region below Stanley Pool'. The grammatical contribution in this little book is of but slight value; 75 of the 267 pages are devoted to 'specimens'

---

1 Cf. 'The Age of Brusciotto' (B.St.Vol.IX, No.2, pp.87-114).
2 Cf. G. Giraud's Vocabulaire des dialectes Sango, Bakongo et A'zandé, page 35; his 'Bakongo' illustrates a mixed riverine commercial type.

of Kongo, and considerable space to word-lists. The grammatical approach is distinctly foreign to Bantu, declensions of nouns by case being illustrated. There is, however, a certain amount of comparative material from other Bantu languages introduced, and an appendix giving a list of works on Bantu languages. Guiness did not himself know Kongo and gleaned his information from two lads who were staying in England with the Rev. Henry Craven. Guiness refers repeatedly to Brusciotto, and he was responsible for the production in the same year (1882) of an English translation of Brusciotto's 'Regulae quaedam'[1]. Guiness refers, in the appendix to his Grammar, to a 'Dictionary of the Congo language (English-Congo, and Congo-English), by Henry Craven, of Livingstone (Congo) Inland Mission, 1882, Hodder and Stoughton, 27 Paternoster Row.' I can find no trace of this publication but have the English-Congo and Congo-English Dictionary by Henry Craven and John Barfield, published in 1883.[2] It is possible that Guiness anticipated a publication which did not materialise until edited the following year by Barfield, who was a tutor at Harley House Institute, Bow. Hodder and Stoughton were the publishers of Guiness' own work. The dictionary of 1883 was a careful piece of work and has an interesting preface in which Barfield refers to Cannecattim's 'list of 1000 Congo words with their Latin and Portuguese equivalents; 600 in Captain Tuckey's "Congo Expedition of 1816"; and 100 more in "Pinkerton's African Travels"'. The incorrect recordings and translations of the two last particularly are exposed. In 1884 Barfield produced The Concords of the Congo Language as spoken at Palaballa.[3] This is, as he states, 'a contribution to the syntax of the Congo tongue', in reality supplementary to Guiness' Grammar. This is a most interesting study of syntax, and deserves more attention than has hitherto been accorded to it. Bentley records[4] that 'the circumstances under which these works were prepared — Craven died about this time — prevented them from being other than provisional'.

The name of W. Holman Bentley will always be remembered for his monumental work on kishiKongo, the Dictionary and Grammar of the Kongo Language, 'as spoken at San Salvador, the Ancient Capital of the Old Kongo Empire'. This large publication of over 700 pages[5] appeared in 1887 and was followed in 1895 by a large Appendix[6] bringing both grammar and dictionary more up to date. Bentley was one of the best-known of the Baptist missionaries in the Congo, and this work of his has remained a standard to today. Taking the main volume and the later appendix together, the 'English-Kongo Dictionary' occupies 345 pages (double col.), the 'Kongo-English Dictionary' 366 pages (double col.), while of the remainder, 290 pages are devoted to grammar. Bentley's 'dictionary' is very reliable, but what he has recorded

---
1 Cf. 'The Age of Brusciotto' (B.St., Vol.IX, No.2, pp.97-8); in 1886 a Portuguese translation by T. da Silva Leitão e Castro appeared.
2 By Harley House, Bow, London; pp.xii + 248 (double col.) + xix.
3 pp.160.
4 Preface (p.xiii) to his 'Dictionary & Grammar of the Kongo Language'.
5 Baptist Missionary Society, pp.xxiv + 718.
6 Bringing the pagination up to 1052.

might have been done more concisely: he has an irritating way of entering the same word repeatedly for each separate meaning, instead of listing the various meanings under a common entry. The grammar is a sound piece of work, and in the appendix the author has added considerably in illustrative sentences and in syntax.

Nils Westlind, Swedish missionary, produced in 1888 his 'Grammatikaliska anmärkningar över kongospråket', in which the central dialects were dealt with. This is a large and important work of 399 pages.

Father Cambier produced in 1891 an Essai sur la langue congolaise at Brussels. In 1895, the Catholic fathers put out a little book in French Eléments de la Langue Congolaise[1], some fifty pages of elementary grammar followed by some pages of phrases and short vocabularies. A work of the same size, title and date is attributed to Delplace (by Starr and Bittremieux). Delplace is also said to have written an Essai d'un dictionnaire Fiote-Français in 1898. In 1901 Father R. Butaye published his Grammaire Kikongo[2], which more or less represents Kibwende and the speech of Leopoldville, and in 1910 his Dictionnaire Kikongo-Français, Français-Kikongo[3]. A fresh editing of this appeared in 1927 entitled Dictionnaire de poche KiKongo-Français, Français-Kikongo, issued by the Mission du Kwango. In 1931 a Petite Grammaire de la langue du Bas-Congo appeared anonymously at Leuven.

Further light, on the comparative side, was given upon Kongo grammatical structure with the publication, in 1903, of W.H. Stapleton's Comparative Handbook of Congo Languages[4]. The scope of this book is given on the title-page, 'a Comparative Grammar of the Eight Principal Languages spoken along the banks of the Congo River from the West Coast of Africa to Stanley Falls, a distance of 1300 miles, and of Swahili, the "lingua franca" of the country stretching thence to the East Coast, with a Comparative Vocabulary giving 800 Selected Words from these Languages with their English equivalents, followed by Appendices on six other Dialects'. Stapleton has done a sound piece of comparative study in this. He consulted all current literature but relied mainly on his personal research with Native speakers for all the languages except KishiKongo, of which he writes: 'of the Lower Congo language, I know practically nothing at first hand, and am greatly indebted to Mr. Bentley for permission to use his work; I have confined my attention to his Grammar and New Testament.' About 1905 E. de Boeck published his Langue congolaise, a little book of 30 pages of reading exercises. In 1907 appeared the third edition of unauthenticated Phrases graduées en Français et en Kikongo ou langue du Bas-Congo, of 67 pages. One of the 'Gaspey-Otto-Sauer' publications was devoted in 1910

---

1 pp.95
2 A new edition entitled Grammaire Congolaise appeared in 1910.
3 I have not seen either of these works; H.H.Johnston records the latter as a 'Kikongo-Swahili-French and Flemish Dictionary' ('Comp.Gram.'Vol. I, p.802). I have followed Laman's record in his 'Kongo Phonology', and that of Bittremieux in his 'Mayombsch Idioticon'.
4 Yakusu, xliii + 326.

to La Langue Congolaise[1], 'grammaire, vocabulaire systématique, phrases graduées et lectures', prepared by A. Seidel and I. Struyf. This is a useful graded study dealing with kishiKongo. Mrs. H.M. Bentley was the authoress in 1911 of a handy well-bound little Guide de Conversation Français-Congolaise[2]. She had previously published (in 1896) a Guide de conversation en Français, Congolais, Portugais, et Hollandais.[3]

We now come to the works of the Swedish missionary K.E. Laman. As early as 1907 he published in Swedish Om Språket i nedre Kongo[4], and in 1912 a considerable grammar entitled Lärobok i Kongo-språket (kiKongo)[5]. This latter contained a short preface by Carl Meinhof, the eminent Bantu scholar. Meinhof's influence is reflected in the full phonetic analysis. The grammar is clearly set forth and gives a clear picture of the phenomena in kiKongo. His English Grammar of the Kongo Language was published in New York in the same year. In 1922 appeared Laman's pioneer work on tone, The Musical Accent or Intonation in the Kongo Language[6]. This work blazed a new trail in Bantu studies. Not only the existence but the importance of tonal recordings was demonstrated and a careful analysis of the forms and function of tone in Kongo was made. The tones were recorded in part by staff musical notation and in part by a variety of diacritical marks. Laman himself later confessed that his treatment was somewhat complicated — "Cet ouvrage étant très étendu et d'une disposition un peu compliquée, il parait au commencement manquer un peu de cohérence et être d'une intelligence difficile".[7] A more concise resumé of the phenomenon was therefore included by him in the preface[8] to his great Kongo dictionary fourteen years later. A further interesting study of Accent in de Kongoleesche talen was contributed to the journal 'Kongo Overzee'[9] in 1937 by A. Burssens and G. van Bulck. This analysed 'accent' in all its aspects, covering the subjects of stress, syllable length and tone. In 1928 Laman collaborated with Meinhof in An Essay on Kongo Phonology which appeared in the 'Z.E.S.'[10] This was a phonetic study in line with Meinhof's other Bantu analyses and dealt with the Central dialects. The 'Essay' was reproduced in 1932 in Meinhof's 'Introduction to the Phonology of the Bantu Languages'[11], the English version of his 'Lautlehre'.

---

1 pp.223.
2 Published by the Ministry of Colonies, Brussels, pp.123. Madame Bentley had previously (in 1902) published a 'Petite grammaire française' in Kongo, in which she included a vocabulaire français-congolais, congolais-français, which was re-issued separately in 1904.
3 pp.188
4 I have not seen a copy of this.
5 Stockholm, pp.xxvi + 336.
6 Stockholm, pp.xviii + 153.
7 'Dictionnaire Kikongo-Français', p.xii.
8 pp.xii — xxxix.
9 Vol.III, pp.113-164, 177-208.
10 Bd. 19, pp.12-40.
11 Ch.VIII 'Kongo', pp.155-175.

Laman's next publication was his Svensk-Kikongo Ordbok[1] of 1931, which paved the way for his monumental Dictionnaire Kikongo-Français[2], published as one of the 'Mémoires' of the 'Institut Royal Colonial Belge' in 1936. This is perhaps the greatest Bantu lexicographical work yet published. It contains nearly 1200 pages (double col.) and between 50,000 and 60,000 entries. Under the term 'Kikongo' it covers a large number of dialects, including the various forms of the Southern kishiKongo, the Western kaKongo, as well as Yombe, Bembe, etc. Throughout the work the author indicated the tones. Nouns are entered under the prefix of the singular, with an indication of the plural where that is necessary. Only a careful selection of derivative forms has been included. This dictionary, one of the best yet produced, lacks however illustrative sentences and idioms, which would probably have increased its size beyond all bounds. The introduction contains a concise phonetic exposition particularly describing the more important dialects. K.E. Laman, who was a missionary in the Congo from 1891, has made a great contribution to the study of Bantu languages, and his name is ever to be associated with Kongo studies. In 1926 P.A. Westlind and E. Karlman produced a little Vocabulaire: Français-Kongo, Kongo-Français of 32 pages. In 1935 L. de Clercq contributed to 'Congo'[3] an article on Le verbe Kikongo, in which he also dealt with Yombe.

(1b) kaKongo is spoken to the north of the Congo mouth area and comprises a number of dialects. The earliest exponent of this form of Kongo was, as we have previously noticed[4], the Abbé Proyart in 1776. Apart from Koelle's vocabularies, the first modern works in this area were by Catholic missionaries of the Mission de Landana, who produced in 1890 a Dictionnaire Français-Fiote (dialecte du Kakongo)[5], while one of their number, Alexandre Visseq, was responsible for a Grammaire Fiote[6] in 1889 and in the same year a Dictionnaire fiot ou dictionnaire de la langue du

---

1 pp.iii, 392.
2 pp.xciv + 1183 (double col.), with map.
3 Vol.II, No.1, pp.1-52.
4 Cf. 'The Age of Brusciotto', pp.105-7.
5 Paris, pp.145 (double col.). F.Starr in his 'A Bibliography of Congo Languages' (1908) entered as No.16 Dictionnaire fiot ou dictionnaire de la langue du Congo, Paris 1889. He notes that he has not seen a copy. He is probably referring to this 1890 publication, which he has fully entered as No.447.
6 pp.64. While Visseq writes in his preface, 'Le présent ouvrage est le premier travail qui ait été fait sur la langue fiote du Congo, depuis des siècles', A. de Clercq in his 'Grammaire du Kiyombe' records a Petite Grammaire de la Langue fiote (dialecte du Loango) pp.88, by A.R. Ussel in 1888, and also a Grammaire de la langue fiote, dialecte du Kakongo by Mgr. Carrie in 1890; I have not seen copies of either of these works. Starr records that the latter has 198 pp.

Congo[1], and Dictionnaire français-fiote[2]; and then a Dictionnaire Fiot-français[3] in 1890. The grammar is a very elementary outline. All these books deal more particularly with the Solongo coastal dialect.

The Vili dialect has been illustrated by the contributions of Chr. Marichelle, who published his Dictionnaire Vili-Français at Loango in 1902, and later his Dictionnaire Français-Vili in 1912 and his Méthode pratique pour l'Etude du Dialecte Vili in 1913.

In 1907 A. de Clercq contributed a descriptive account of Yombe grammar in his Grammaire du Kiyombe published in 'Ant.'[4] A more up-to-date treatment, with an improved orthography, has been provided by L. de Clercq in his Grammaire du Kiyombe[5] of 1921. Yombe has further been illustrated by the publications of L. Bittremieux, the author of Mayombsch Idioticon[6], the first two volumes of which appeared in 1922, and the third, a supplementary volume, in 1927. This is a very considerable Yombe dictionary with explanations in Dutch, and a large amount of cyclopaedic information. It is of great linguistic value and includes much illustrative textual and idiomatic material. Bittremieux published (in 1912) an interesting lexical study of personal names, under the title of Mayombsche Namen; this was later improved and republished in 1934.[7]

(2) Ndongo (generally erroneously referred to as kiMbundu), spoken in Northern Angola from Loanda to Benguela. In order to keep it distinct from uMbundu, which belongs to the Western Bantu Zone, the old and indigenous term[8] Ndongo should be used. It has already been observed that the second Bantu book known to have been published, de Couto's Gentio de Angola[9] of 1643, was in this language. In 1697 appeared Dias' Arte da lingua de Angola[10], the second known Bantu Grammar, while the works of Cannecattim of 1804 and 1805 have already been noted.[11]

---

1 pp. iv + 156. I have not seen a copy of this.
2 pp. 156. I have not seen a copy of this.
3 pp. 212 (double col.).
4 Vol. II, pp. 449-466, 761-794.
5 No. 5 of the series Bibliothèque-Congo, pp. 95.
6 Congo-Bibliotheek, Nos. 10, 11 and 21, pp. 918.
7 He further contributed to the journal 'Congo' in 1925 and 1926, Onomatopee en werkwoord in 't Kongoleesch, in which he demonstrated, especially from Yombe, the importance of this class of words (which we now call the 'ideophone'), but he pointed out that they were particularly used by the 'unlettered'.
8 J. C. Prichard, in his 'Researches into the Physical History of Mankind', 2nd edition 1826, refers to the 'Dongo People' (Vol. I. p. 533); and Pacconio and de Couto in the 'Gentio de Angola' also refer to 'Ndongo' in § 11 of the 'Observationes' prefaced to the 2nd edition of 1661.
9 Cf. 'The Age of Brusciotto', p. 89.
10 Cf. 'The Age of Brusciotto', p. 103.
11 Cf. 'The Age of Brusciotto', p. 110.

Héli Chatelain gives a bibliography of Ndongo literature in his 'Folk-Tales of Angola'[1] printed in 1894. From this I cull the following information concerning works published during the latter half of the Nineteenth Century: In 1864 Dr. Saturnino de Souza e Oliveira and M.A. de Castro Francina published Elementos grammaticaes da lingua nbundu at Loanda. 'Written by a Brazilian doctor, assisted by an educated Native, this work is slightly better than that of Cannecattim; but it is as short and rare as Pedro Dias' work, which surpasses it in grammatical value. In 1864, Dr. Saturnino de Souza e Oliveira began the publication of his Diccionario da lingua n'bundu. A large part or the whole was printed, but never stitched, and only a few unique manuscript slips and printed pages of this valuable work are left.

'Vocabularies of Ki-Mbundu have been collected by Dr. Livingstone, of whose work an unpublished copy exists in the Grey Library, Cape Town; by the German explorer Lux, published as an appendix to his book[2], and by the Brazilian Dutra. The vocabulary of the latter was published without the author's name, as an appendix to Capello and Ivens' book 'De Benguella ás terras de Iacca', Lisboa, 1881. In 1887 it was republished, and again without the author's name, by the then Bishop of Angola and Congo, Don Antonio Leitão e Castro. The original manuscript is, for the present, in my possession. About 1883 Sebastião de Jesus completed a Diccionario n'bundo, which was not without value, but the author died before he could find a publisher. It still exists in manuscript[3], but is not worth publishing now.'

In addition to the above, H.H. Johnston mentions[4] a vocabulary by Hale published in a report of the United States Naval Expedition to Southwest Africa in 1846.

The one great authority on this language is, however, the distinguished Swiss Missionary Dr. Héli Chatelain, who died in 1908. A naturalised American citizen, he went to Loanda in 1885 'as pioneer and linguist of Bishop William Taylor's self-supporting missions in Africa.' His 'duty was to acquire the languages, impart them to the Missionaries, and prepare grammars, vocabularies, translations and other elementary books needed by Missionaries in the course of their labors'. Chatelain's linguistic gifts were very considerable; he was acquainted with French and German, his two native languages, and also English, Italian, Spanish, Greek, Latin and Hebrew. He was, however, handicapped by the self-supporting scheme, and had to study Portuguese and keep himself by private tuition.[5] Apart from his well-known book of Folk-tales, his outstanding contribution in this area is his Grammatica Elementar do Kimbundu[6], a thoroughly competent

---

1 pp.23-25.
2 in 1880.
3 H.H. Johnston also refers to a MS. dictionary by Joaquim d'Almeida da Cunha.
4 'Comparative Study', Vol.I, p.801.
5 Apart from learning several Bantu languages, Chatelain also mastered Afrikaans, spoken by the Boer settlers in Angola.
6 pp.xxiv, 174.

work in Portuguese, but with an English rendering of the examples. This work which appeared in 1889 was a graded study with practical exercises. A German edition, <u>Grundzüge des Kimbundu oder der Angola-Sprache</u>[1] appeared the same year, without the practical exercises, but 'enriched by many additional notes, and by tables comparing Ki-mbundu with the six principal West Central African languages.' In 1889 Chatelain had also published in the 'Z.A.S.' Vocabularies of Mbamba and 'Umbangala' (with translation in Portuguese, English, German and Ndongo)[2].

Chatelain also lists three works by an educated Native, J.D.Cordeiro da Matta, a collection of proverbs and riddles with Portuguese translation in 1891, a 'Ki-Mbundu' Primer in 1892, and his <u>Ensaio de Diccionario Kimbundu-Portuguez</u>[3] in 1893, which Chatelain considers to be the best vocabulary of the language published up to that time. We have no information of more recent Ndongo studies.

(3) <u>North-eastern Congo</u>: <u>Kele</u>[4] is spoken on both banks of the Congo and Lomami Rivers near their junction. <u>So</u> (referred to linguistically as 'Soko' and 'Heso' — the people being 'Baso') is spoken in the region of the Aruwimi River mouth. Very little scientific work has been done upon these languages. Both are illustrated in Stapleton's 'Comparative Handbook of Congo Languages' (1903), and both contribute elements to Dr. A. Sims' <u>Yalulema Vocabulary</u>[5] of 1887. In 1906 Stapleton contributed in the 'Journal of the African Society' a short <u>Note on the Kele Verb</u>; while the Baptist missionaries at Yakusu are responsible for some little booklets, e.g. <u>Prefatory Grammar Notes</u>[6] on Kele, and <u>Un Vocabulaire Français-Lokele</u>;[7] and in typescript a grammar by W.H. Ford and an interesting work <u>The Tonetics of the Lokele Language</u>[8] by J.F. Carrington, elaborated in 1943 in his <u>Tonal Structure of Kele (Lokele)</u>.[9]

(4) <u>Middle Congo</u>: All the main languages of this group are illustrated in Stapleton's 'Comparative Handbook of Congo Languages' (1903).

(a) <u>Poto</u> is spoken along the northernmost part of the Congo River between the Mongala and the Itimbiri. No linguistic work seems to have been done in this language apart from a vocabulary of 'Upoto'

---

1 Reprinted from the 'Z.A.S.', 1889, pp.265-314.
2 Vol.2, pp.109-136, <u>Bemerkungen über die Sammlung von Mbamba-Wörter und über das Mbamba-Volk</u>, Vol.2, pp.136-146, <u>Bemerkungen zu der Sammlung von Umbangala-Wörter</u>.
3 pp.xiv, 174; see also the notice of this author and his works in Lit. Centralbl., 1893, p.40, by Schuchardt.
4 This type of Kele is loKele.
5 pp.35.
6 pp.16.
7 pp.12 (double col.).
8 1940; pp.19 (quarto.)
9 'African Studies', Vol.II, pp.193-209.

in H.H. Johnston's 'Uganda Protectorate', and Stapleton's comparative work. Poto is now spoken by a mere handful of people in one community.

(b) Ngombe dialects are spoken in several different areas both north and south of the northernmost bend of the Congo River. Maes and Boone in 'Les Peuplades du Congo Belge' (pp.239-240), give five areas as follows: '1°) dans la région de la Lua supérieure, aux environs de Bosobolo; 2°) dans la région s'étandant de Bomboma à Akula sur la Mongala; 3°) dans la Lulonga et l'Ikelemba inférieures; 4°) sur la rive gauche de la Lomela; 5°) sur la rive gauche du fleuve Congo et la Lopori supérieure'. The first work of scientific importance which appeared on this language was M. Guilmin's Grammaire Lingombe[1] published at New Antwerp in 1925. In 1937 E.A. and L. Ruskin produced their Notes on the Grammar of Lingombe, some 60 pages with 150 pages of Vocabularies. This work owes much to earlier work in manuscript by W.H.White, Miss Cork, Mrs.W.Forfeitt and J. Davidson. The Tonal Structure of the Ngombe Verb by E.W. Price is a short paper contributed to 'African Studies' in 1944.

(c) Mongo[2] may be considered as the principal of a cluster of closely allied languages including Nkundu. Early writers used the term Lolo for the language spoken between the Lulonga-Maringa river system and the Tshuapa River in the south; Mongo proper lies east of this to the Lopori River; while Nkundu, to the south, extends almost as far as the Lukenie River. Stapleton in 1903 stated[3]: 'How far the dialect of Lolo given in this book (generally known as Lu-nkundu) reaches is not known, but it is probable that Lolo in its different dialects is spoken by a greater number of people (with the possible exception of Ngombe) than is any other Upper River language'.

In 1887 J.B. Eddie published 'A Vocabulary of Kilolo, as spoken by the Bankundu, a section of the Balolo tribe at Ikengo (Equator), Upper Congo'. This[4] contained a few introductory notes on the grammar. From this Miss L.M. de Hailes of the Congo Balolo Mission compiled her little Kilolo-English Vocabulary[5] of 1891. In 1893 appeared A Guide to the Luñkundu Language, prepared by J. and F.T.McKittrick[6]. A second edition[7], corrected and enlarged, was issued in 1897. The actual grammatical lessons are of the slightest; the main body of the book is made up of conversations, passages for reading and then vocabularies, with a vocabulary of Mongo added. In 1903 A. & L. Ruskin

---

1 Referred to by Burssens. I have not seen this.
2 Reference may be made to the particulars and maps given by Maes and Boone in 'Les Peuplades du Congo Belge' pp.103-4, 246-249, 291-2.
3 'Comparative Handbook of Congo Languages', page 9 of introduction.
4 pp. v + 203.
5 pp.159.
6 pp. iv + 230.
7 pp. iv + 266, with additional blank pages for notes.

produced Outlines of the Grammar of the Lomóngo Language[1], a concise little exposition of the salient points of the grammar. Naturally terminology and classification are of the 'old style'. In 1913 A. F. Hensey produced in a large work of 427 pages his English-Lonkundo and Lonkundo-English Vocabulary. In 1914 Mr. Eldred published Lonkundo-Français, being Lessons in French, a little book of 35 pages. In 1917 appeared E.R. Moon's First Lessons in Lo-Nkundo, of 73 pages. Mr. & Mrs. Ruskin made a valuable contribution to Bantu linguistic studies in 1928, when they published A Dictionary of the Lomongo Language[2]. The first section, pp.1-146, is 'Lomongo-English-French' and the second, pp.347-651, is 'English-Lomongo'. It is an extensive record of the language containing much idiomatic material, and recording numerous ideophones, which the authors treat as 'indeclinable adverbs, derived from verbs'. Some, of course, such as kombe from komba are formed from verbs, but the greater number, such as kombo, form the basis of verbs(e.g. kombola). Bibliographies of the Musée du Congo Belge make reference to two works by Verpoorten, published at 'Gand' before 1930: Grammaire Lokundo (92 pp.) and Vocabulaire Lokundo (106 pp.). I have not seen either of these. A valuable study of the grammar of this group appeared with the publication in 1938 of G. Hulstaert's Praktische Grammatica van het Lonkundo (Lomongo)[3]. Tone changes are carefully recorded and consistently marked. Hulstaert had already made a special study of tone in his 'Ant.' article Les Tons en Lonkundo, and in his article in 'Kongo-Overzee' (1935) Over de tonen in het Lonkundo. This grammar, while stereotyped European methods and nomenclature are retained, is framed for practical ends, being arranged with a series of graded exercises replete with valuable idiomatic examples. In 1939 he contributed a valuable study dealing with tonetics, Spraakleer van het Lonkundo[4].

Closely parallel to Mongo is Ntomba, spoken by a people to the west of the Nkundu, on the eastern side of Lake Leopold II and the southern shores of Lake Tumba. For our knowledge of this language we are indebted to two publications by L. Gilliard, his Grammaire Synthétique de Lontomba[5] and his Grammaire Pratique Lontomba[6], both of 1928. The former contains a short exposition (pp.45) of the grammar followed by extensive vocabularies (Français-Lontomba, pp.82, and Lontomba-Français, pp.167). The 'practical' grammar is set up in the form of exercises. Much about the same time American Baptist Missionaries were using a little cyclostyled Suggestions for

---

1 pp.xii + 76.
2 By E.A. & L. Ruskin, Christian Literature Society, pp. viii + 651 (double col.); the authors refer to 'Mrs. Mackenzie's Grammar of Mongo' and 'Mr. Hensey's Vocabulary of Mongo'.
3 Published at Antwerp, pp.viii + 272.
4 Published by: De Sikkel.
5 pp.304.
6 pp.92.

a LoNtomba Grammar, quarto, pp.29, in which the elements were set out.

Also allied are the Kuba (or Bushongo), Tetela (or 'Tetela – Nkutshu') and Kela languages, though the exact relationship of these has not yet been determined. Certain spasmodic contributions upon some of these have been made. Regarding Kuba, P.Denolf contributed to 'Congo'[1] in 1932 Lukuba, Taal der Bakuba, in 't bizonder de gewesttaal der Mpianga, which included a small vocabulary of 'Tshiluba–Vlaamsch–Bakuba'. In the same year A.B. Edmiston published a large Grammar and Dictionary of the Bushonga or Bukuba Language. The grammatical section of this (pp.1–209) is fairly full and was based in method upon Morrison's work in Luba–Lulua. The dictionary part (pp.213–619) constitutes a valuable section. Linguistic evidence, as well as what Torday observes, bears out the theory that these people were originally of Sudanic origin but have adopted a Bantu language — they still have remnants of the old non–Bantu 'Lumbila' tongue. For Tetela, P. van Hove contributed to 'Ant.'[2] in 1911 a short Esquisse de la langue des Wankutshu, and E.Handekyn a Spraakkunst der Wankutshu-taal to 'Congo'[3] in 1927.

(d) Ngala, as a pure Bantu tongue is spoken on the north and south banks of the Gongo River between 18°30' and 21° East longitude. This language is today called 'Lingala', though it is based on the speech of the Mangala people.[4] The influence of this language has extended over a great part of Northern Congoland in a mixed and corrupt form which goes under the designation of 'Bangala'. As early as 1891 Cambier treated of the Ngala of Limboko area in his Essais sur la langue congolaise[5]. This was also dealt with by Stapleton in his 'Comparative Handbook' in 1903; but in the same year Stapleton published Suggestions pour une Grammaire du 'Bangala' (La 'lingua franca' du Haut Congo)[6], in which he recognised the growth of the mixed commercial and administrative language, and attempted to retard its downward progress by presenting and advocating grammatical rules to preserve its Bantu character. An English translation of this book was issued the same year.[7] Meanwhile E. de Boeck put out in

---

1 Vol.XVIII.
2 Vol.VI, pp.385–402.
3 Vol.VIII, pp.52–61, 215–230, 377–399.
4 An informative discussion of the position of this language is contributed by J.Tanghe in his Le Lingala, la langue du fleuve, in the Review 'Congo', Oct.1930, pp.1–18.
5 pp.viii + 124.
6 B.M.S. Yakusu, j + 146, containing phrases and a vocabulary of some 2000 words; a new edition appeared in 1911 with the title 'Propositions', instead of 'Suggestions'.
7 Second edition in 1914 'revised and enlarged by Frank Longland'; grammar pp.1–50, vocabularies and phrases pp.51–178.

1904 his Grammaire et Vocabulaire du 'Bangala' ou Langue du Haut-Congo[1], following this with two publications dealing with the real 'liNgala', Notions du Lingala ou langue du Haut-fleuve[2], and Lingala: Petit vocabulaire et phrases usuelles[3]. In 1908 appeared 'Bangala',Langue Commerciale du Haut-Congo[4], by A.Courboin, a manual of conversation, including a few pages of very elementary grammar. In this 'Bangala' is given as it is spoken, not as language students would like to hear it spoken, and the picture one gets of it is of a language approaching the 'pidgin' stage, though still much more Bantu in its construction than the 'Kitchen Kafir' of South Africa. In 1910 Capt.T.C.Mackenzie published, through the Intelligence Department of the Sudan Government at Cairo, a very small Vocabulary of the Bangala Language[5], as spoken in the Lado District, Mongalla Province. Some phrases are included. In 1926 C. Elge published at Antwerp his little Dictionnaire Bangala-Français-Flamand[6] in three sections: (1) 'Français-Bangala', (2) 'Vlaamsch-Bangala', (3) 'Bangala-français-Flamand'. Elge also wrote, in Nederlands and French, Eenige Begrippen van Lingala, met Woordenlijst en gebruikelijke Volzinnen (undated). The 'Missionnaires de Scheut' published a handy little Vocabulaire Lingala-Français, Français-Lingala[7], which has had wide use. Three publications came out in 1927: E. de Boeck's Cours théorique et pratique de Lingala, avec vocabulaire et phrases usuelles; a publication without author's name, Eléments de la Grammaire Bangala de l'Uelé, suivis d'un vocabulaire; and van Mol's Bangala Spraakleer met Woordenlijst[8]. In 1928 E.Rubben contributed an important study of the language in his Leçons pratiques de lingala, a book of 257 pages, which I have not seen. In 1939 Malcolm Guthrie, a missionary of the B.M.S., put students of Bantu in his debt by a splendid little treatise entitled Grammaire et Dictionnaire de Lingala (la langue universelle actuellement parlée sur les deux rives de la partie centrale du fleuve Congo)[9]. This is a careful analysis of the riverine language in its true Bantu form. The orthography is carefully worked out. There is an exposition of intonation and the tones are marked throughout the grammatical, dictionary and conversational parts of the book. He had previously (in 1935) edited, in English, a Lingala Grammar and Dictionary[10], of which the

---

1 pp.163.
2 pp.38, 1904.
3 pp.31, 1906.
4 pp.ix + 146; another edition (also undated) is pp.367 (9.5 x 14cms).
5 pp.47.
6 pp.227.
7 pp.344. The copy I have consulted is a 2nd edition undated.
8 pp.153.
9 pp.x+191; grammar pp.1-77; French-Lingala Dictionary, pp.81-127; Lingala-French Dictionary, pp.131-160; Manual of Conversation pp.165-189.
10 The results of the work of a Committee of Missionaries, J.H. Marker, D.C. Davies, W.H. Edwards and A.B. Palmer, called at Yalemba in 1931. This contained 59 pages of Grammar and 170 pages of Vocabularies.

'Grammaire' is a revised French version. Guthrie further contributed an article to the 'B.S.O.S.' on Tone Ranges in a Two-Tone Language (Lingala) in 1940.[1] There are several dialectal forms of 'Ngala', of one of which, Mabale, J. Tanghe has given some textual examples, but no grammatical analysis. For Buja dialect there are I. Schillebeeckx's Grammaire et Vocabulaire Lingala-Budja of 1925 and L. Toulmond's Essai de grammaire d'Ebudja, which appeared in 'Congo'[2] in 1937. Mention might also be made of a 1916 publication, Welle Tutor and Vocabulary (no author's name given).

(e) Bangi, also called 'Yanzi' are found in two distinct areas: (1) on the left bank of the Congo between Lake Tumba and the Kwa mouth of the Kasai, and in French Equatorial Africa on the opposite bank of the Congo, where they occupy a vast territory of the basins and watersheds of the Alima and Sanga Rivers; and (2) in the triangle formed by the confluence of the Kasai and Kwango Rivers.

A. Sims was the author of A Vocabulary of Kibangi 'as spoken by the Babangi (commonly called Bayansi) on the Upper Congo from Kwa mouth (Kasai) to Liboko (Bangala)', in 1886[3]. In 1899 appeared J. Whitehead's well-known Grammar and Dictionary of the Bobangi Language[4], which is the main authority we have for this language. Most of the book is devoted to fairly comprehensive vocabularies, and only 80 pages to the grammatical part. Whitehead recognised the existence and importance of tone, but the indication of this by diacritic marks in addition to their use to shew modified quality in vowels produced a very difficult orthography. For instance low tone was generally indicated by a bar above the vowel, but in the case of the 'modified' vowels ê and ô, they were read thus as of low tone and indicated ë and ö if of high tone; e thus appeared as e, ē, ê, ë and even é if a 'raised' tone needed specifically to be marked. Stapleton treated of the language in his 'Comparative Handbook'; but little further attention has been paid to its scientific study since Whitehead's publication.

In 1940 A.G.W. MacBeath published Bobangi in Twenty-one Lessons[5], a practical book with Exercises and Key. In it were included many ideophones under the name of 'indeclinables'. It is based on Whitehead's work.

---

1 'B.S.O.S.' Vol.X, pp.469-478.
2 pp.361-376, 481-525.
3 pp.xi, 111. Sims is further credited with a Handbook of Bobangi (1888-89), but I have no definite particulars of this. (Cf. Starr's 'Bibliography', No.490; and Whitehead's Grammar, Preface p.vi.)
4 pp.xix + 499.
5 pp.iv + 103.

Regarding the Dzing dialect, J.Mertens devoted the second part of his <u>Les Ba Dzing de la Kamtsha</u> (1938) to a study of the grammar of the language.

(5) <u>Teke</u>: spoken on right bank of the Congo over a large area of French Equatorial Africa from the Alima River to the Djoué and around Stanley Pool. There are numerous dialectal types of this illustrated in Koelle's 'Polyglotta Africana'. The 'Itio' or real Teke dialect is illustrated in A.Sims' <u>Vocabulary of the Kiteke</u> 'as spoken by the Bateke (Batio) and kindred Tribes on the Upper Congo', (2 vols)[1] published in 1888. The 'Ifumu' or Eastern Teke is illustrated by Father J.Calloch in his <u>Vocabulaire Français-Ifumu (Batéké)</u>[2], with a grammatical sketch in 1911; and in his <u>Manuel de Conversation de la langue itékée (Brazzaville)</u> he dealt with kiSantu. In 1927 K.E. Laman contributed to the 'Festschrift Meinhof'[3] an article on <u>The Musical Tone of the Teke Language</u>.

(6) <u>Bira</u>, or Kumu-Bira, spoken in the Belgian Congo to the west of Lake Albert. For this group we have Aloys' <u>Vocabulaire Kikumu-Kifransa</u>, printed at Stanleyville, undated; two short notes in 'Kongo-Overzee' by L.Maeyens: <u>De bilabiale, stemhebbende implosief in het kiBira</u>[4], and <u>Het inlandsch Lied en het Muzikaal Accent met semantische functie bij de Babira</u>[5], both published in 1938. In 1939 C. Meinhof published in the 'Z.E.S.'[6] an informative article, <u>Die Sprache der Bira</u>, dealing with phonology and grammar.

(7) <u>Bua</u>, or Bwale, with dialect Ngelima amongst others, is spoken on the south bank of the Welle River, 24°–26° E. and from 2°–3.50°N. The people are surrounded by Sudanic Azande, and the language is no doubt influenced thereby, as it is an extreme type. In 1924 P.Gérard published at Brussels <u>La langue Lebéo, grammaire et vocabulaire</u>, dealing with this language. A. de Calonne-Beaufaict in his <u>Les Ababua</u> (undated) devoted pp.410–451 to grammatical notes and a vocabulary of 'Libwâlé'.

[4] CENTRAL ZONE

<u>Position</u>: Central, Eastern and Southern Congo and Northern Rhodesia, roughly bounded by Angola on the west, Lake Tanganyika on the east, 4° south latitude in the north and the Zambesi Valley in the south.

---

1 'An English-Kiteke Vocabulary', pp.190 (single col.), 1886; and 'A Kiteke-English Vocabulary', pp.160 (single col.).
2 pp.iv, 346.
3 pp.118–124.
4 Vol.IV, 1, pp.23, 24.
5 Vol.IV, 5, pp.250–259.
6 Band XXIX, Heft 4, pp.241–287.

Characteristics: The main distinguishing features of this zone are:

(i) The occurrence of both monosyllabic and disyllabic prefix forms.
(ii) Noun classes to indicate augmentative, diminutive and locative forms (including the purest Bantu type of locative).
(iii) A relatively simple type of phonology.
(iv) Basic uninfluenced phonetic combinations.
(v) A certain degree of vowel and nasal harmony.
(vi) A high development of verbal derivatives.
(vii) A high development of ideophones.
(viii) A three-tone system.

The most important languages[1] in this zone may be roughly classified as follows:

(1) Luba group:
    (a) Luba, with numerous dialectal varieties: Lulua, Sanga, Kaonde, Hemba, Luna-Inkongo, Songe.
    (b) Luunda (of Kambove).
    (c) Kanyoka.
    (d) Nkoya, Mbwera.

(2) Bemba group:
    (a) Bemba, dials. Tabwa, Mambwe, Lungu.
    (b) Aushi.
    (c) Lamba, dials. Ŵulima, Seŵa, Luano.
    (d) Bisa.
    (e) Lala, dial. Maswaka.
    (f) Namwanga.
    (g) Fipa.

(3) Tonga group:
    (a) Tonga, dials. Northern & Southern, We, Totela.
    (b) Ila, dials. Lundwe, Mala.
    (c) Mukuni (or Lenje), dial. Twa.

(4) Zambesi group (allied to Tonga):
    (a) Subiya.
    (b) Luyi.
    (c) Leya.

---

[1] Many languages upon which there is no literature available are omitted from this classification. Further knowledge may make it essential to include a number of these.

(1) Luba Group.

(a) **Luba**: This large cluster of languages stretches over a vast area of Central and Southern Belgian Congo from Angola to Tanganyika. The many varieties have not yet been fully studied with a view to any unification, but they are found in the districts of Kasai, Sankuru, Lomami, Lulua, Tanganyika-Moero, Manyema and Haut-Luapula. Mgr.de Clercq writes of it[1], 'Ainsi donc, le Tshiluba se trouve être la plus répandue de toutes les langues indigènes du Congo Belge'. Burssens distinguishes between '**kiLuva**' of the Katanga and '**t∫iLuba**' or '**bu-Luba**' of the Kasai, and divides the speakers of the latter into (1) Western Baluba (listing 21 tribal names), (2) the Bena-Luluwa, and (3) the Bena-Konji.[2]

In considering the literature dealing with this cluster we find ourselves faced with the following divisions treated: (i) Western, Luba-Lulua; (ii) Eastern, Luba-Hemba; (iii) Southern, Luba-Sanga; (iv) Northern, Luna-Inkongo; (v) Central,'Luba commune'; (vi) Songe of the North, and (vii) Kaonde of the South.

Of the Western type, that of Luba-Lulua, the earliest study we have is A. Jannsens' Eléments du dialecte Muluba, Haut Kassai, of 185 pages, published by the Mouvement géographique in 1895. Two years later appeared A. de Clercq's Grammaire de la langue Bena-Lulua.[3] In 1906 W.M. Morrison of the American Presbyterian Congo Mission published his Grammar and Dictionary of the Buluba-Lulua language as spoken in the Upper Kasai and Congo Basin[4], a work of very considerable merit. A revision of the grammatical part, brought up-to-date in spelling, was published by a 'Committee on revision' in 1930, entitled Grammar of the Buluba-Lulua Language[5]. T.C.Vinson had prepared and published[6] a supplement to the dictionary part of Morrison's work, and a dictionary committee, consisting of V.A. Anderson, W.F.McElroy and G.T. McKee, issued an enlarged dictionary, in 1939, entitled Dictionary of the Tshiluba Language[7], containing both Luba-English and English-

---

1 A. de Clercq in his 'Grammaire pratique de la langue Luba', of 1911.
2 A. Burssens in 'Africa' Vol.XII, pp.267-8.
3 Brussels, 1897, pp.vii+110; I have not seen a copy either of this or of Jannsens' work. They are listed by Starr as Nos.200 and 310 respectively in his 'Bibliography of Congo Languages'. De Clercq also wrote a four-page pamphlet in Z.A.O.S., 1900.
4 pp.x+417; in 1914 Morrison published a Simplified Grammar of the Baluba Language, 26 pages only; he was also responsible for a Luba-Lulua Exercise Book of 50 pages.
5 pp. x + 189.
6 in 1918.
7 pp. vi + 134 + 173.

Luba sections. These publications give a very clear picture of the western type of Luba. Other works on Western Luba include A.C. McKinnon's Dictionnaire Français-Buluba, Buluba-Français[1] printed at Luebo in 1929; and L.Achten's Vocabulaire des Populations de la Région du Kasai-Lulua-Sankuru, published by J. Maes in the 'Journal de la Société des Africanistes'[2] in 1934. Two small works have been published on the Kete dialect: D.W. Snyder's Kikete Primer of 1895, and A. de Clercq's Esquisse de la langue Bakete of 1898, contributed to the 'Z.A.O.S.' (Vol.IV, pp.316-336).

For the Eastern type, Luba-Hemba, we have two publications by J. Vandermeiren, viz. Grammaire de la langue Kiluba-Hemba[3] (1912) and Vocabulaire: Kiluba Hemba-Français, Français-Kiluba Hemba[4] (1913). These are very handy little books of practical size[5] published by the Ministère des Colonies, Bruxelles.

Southern Luba, Luba-Sanga of the Katanga district, was first exemplified by C.A. Swan of the Garenganze Mission in his Notes on the Grammatical Construction of Chiluba in 1892. This rare little item was made up of a brief grammatical outline of 20 pages, followed by 32 pages of vocabularies (either way) and a translation of the first six chapters of John's Gospel. In 1908 J.M.Jenniges produced a little work in French, Traité de Kiluba-Sanga[6], a brief grammatical outline published by the Etat Indépendant du Congo; and in the following year appeared a Dictionnaire Français-Kiluba by Emile Jenniges; I have not seen this. About the year 1911 J.A. Clarke prepared a Luba-Sanga Grammar. This was produced in a number of roneod copies[7] for the use of missionaries of the Garenganze Mission. It is a painstaking piece of work and of considerable reference value, consisting of three parts, Grammar (pp.1-146), Idiomatic phrases and folk texts (pp.1-17, 1-6), and English-Luba-Sanga Vocabulary (pp.1-51). In 1915 Clarke published from Madras his English Chi-luba-Sanga Vocabulary[8], which comprised parts II and III of the previous work preceded by a few pages of grammatical notes and tables. Clarke also produced a book of 'French Ki-Luba Exercises' and a book of 'Vocabulary and Phrases'. Another little book on this dialect was First Lessons in Kiluba[9] by H. Womersley of the Congo Evangelistic

---

1 pp.208
2 Paris: Vol.IV, No.2, pp.211 et seq.
3 pp.302.
4 pp.1046; Luba-Français occupying pp.15-276 (single col.), and Français-Luba pp.279-1046 (double col.).
5 14 x 8.5cms.
6 pp.44.
7 Koni Hill, Katanga; pp.230 quarto, typed.
8 pp.127.
9 pp.vi + 66.

Mission, printed in 1932. In 1937 H. Roland produced a <u>Grammaire de la langue Kisanga</u>[1], and in the following year a <u>Vocabulaire Français-Kisanga</u>. I have seen neither of these.

Another Southern dialect of Luba is the <u>Kaonde</u> of North-western Rhodesia, and of this R.E. Broughall Woods, a Native Commissioner, published in 1924 <u>A Short Introductory Dictionary of the Kaonde Language, with English-Kaonde Appendix</u>[2]. This is quite a useful vocabulary but hardly worthy of the title of 'dictionary'.

Of <u>Luna-Inkongo</u> or Northern Luba we have only W.H. Westcott's <u>Concise Grammar of Luna Inkongo</u>[3], a very sketchy outline, published in Bristol, undated; but in another Northern type, <u>Songe</u>, A. Samain published, about 1923, as No. XIV of the 'Bibliothèque-Congo' <u>La Langue Kisonge, Grammaire, Vocabulaire, Proverbes</u>[4], a short but reliable compendium.

There have been movements towards the recognition of a Central type of Luba, one which will simplify administrative contacts. This has been referred to as '<u>Luba commune</u>'. As early as 1889 C.G. Büttner had made a fourteen-page contribution <u>Zur Grammatik der Balubasprache</u> to the 'Z.A.S.'[5]; but the most notable contribution was made by A. de Clercq who published in 1903 his <u>Grammaire de la langue Luba</u>, a large work of over 500 pages[6], of which pp. 151-313 are devoted to a 'Vocabulaire Luba-Français', and pp. 315-504 to a 'Vocabulaire Français-Luba'. In 1911 de Clercq produced his <u>Grammaire pratique de la langue Luba</u>[7], a class book, and in 1929 his <u>Nouvelle Grammaire Luba</u>[8], framed for the assistance of those who have daily contact with the Natives but do not require an academic knowledge of the language. In writing of the language treated de Clercq says: 'Ce n'est pas le dialecte d'une région déterminée; c'est plutôt la langue commune qui, de par la fréquence des communications entre les Noirs des diverses régions, et de par la compénétration des tribus, s'est formée tout naturellement.' In 1914 de Clercq had published his big <u>Dictionnaire Luba: Luba-Français, Français-Luba</u>[9], a book of nearly 600 pages. This was later re-issued in two volumes, 'Luba-Français'[10] in 1936, and 'Français-Luba'[11] in 1937. Mention

---

1 pp. 111.
2 pp. 234; Kaonde-English 1-180, English-Kaonde 183-234.
3 pp. 98.
4 pp. 152, of which only 24 pages are devoted to grammar, 108 being devoted to the Vocabulaire Français-Kisonge.
5 Vol. II, pp. 220-33.
6 Brussels, pp. vi, 7 + 504; I have not seen this.
7 pp. 2 + vi + 151; a 24-page supplement was added in 1920.
8 pp. 102.
9 Brussels: pp. vii + 583.
10 Leopoldville, pp. vii + 307.
11 Leopoldville, pp. vi + 274.

might here be made of a short article by de Clercq on Le Verbe en langue Luba which appeared in 'Congo'[1] in 1925.

Quite a number of other publications on Luba have appeared, and mention might be made of the contributions of Frère Gabriel (Vermeersch). In 1921 he produced his Etude du Tshiluba[2], containing a 'Luba-French' vocabulary. Reprints have appeared, including a fourth edition of the grammatical part: Etude des langues congolaises bantoues avec applications au Tshiluba.[3] The vocabulary portion appeared later as Dictionnaire Tshiluba-Français[4]. In the same year, 1921, he published at Brussels his Dictionnaire Français-Kiluba.[5] Brother Gabriel's work is highly rated. H.Quinot in 1926 wrote a Petite Grammaire de la langue Kiluba (Tshiluba) du Congo Belge (Province du Kasai) of 35 pages; and in the same year a Vocabulaire français-kiswahili-kiluba du Congo belge of 91 pages. In 1927 came van Scheut's Petit vocabulaire Tshiluba-Français of 123 pages; and in 1928 A. Verbeken's Abrégé de Grammaire Tshiluba of 60 pages. An undated, uncredited publication, issued from Lusambo, Imprimerie Ecole Professionelle, of 200 pages was the polyglot Vocabulaire, Français-Kituba-Tshiluba-Tshisonge-Tshikuba-Tshitetela, dealing with a number of Congo languages belonging to various groups.

In the modern study of Luba the recently-established[6] journal 'Kongo-Overzee' has played a large part. In this the pioneer worker A. de Clercq contributed his Lubataal-Studie to Vols.I and II. In the realm of phonology and tonology A. Burssens made a number of valuable contributions between 1936 and 1939[7]. Further contributions have been made by him in conjunction with S. Peeraer. In 1939 he contributed Le Tʃílúbà, Langue à Intonation to 'Africa'[8]. Burssens' greatest work, however, was his monograph, Tonologische Schets van het Tshiluba (Kasayi, Belgisch Kongo)[9], published in 1939 at Antwerp.

---

1 Vol.VI, pp.723-730.
2 pp.xv + 297.
3 Turnhout, undated, pp.155.
4 Brussels, undated, pp.v + 134.
5 pp.ii + 241.
6 Vol.2, under the editorship of Dr. Amaat Burssens of the University of Ghent, appeared in 1934.
7 Het Tshiluba en de phonologische 'Africa' Spelling (1936); Tonologisch Onderzoek van het Luba: Het 'Hoofdtelwoord' (1938); Het Partikel —A in het tshiLuba (1938); Tonologisch Onderzoek van de copula DI in het tshiLuba (1938); Tonologisch Onderzoek van het Aanwijzend Woord in het tshiLuba (1939); Tonologisch Onderzoek van het Substitutieve Pronomen in het tshiLuba (1939); Linguistisch Onderzoek in Centraal-Katanga; het kiLuba als Toontaal (1939); etc.
8 Vol.XII No.3, pp.267-284.
9 pp.xiv + 232.

This is a fine grammatical study of the language on a thorough tonetic basis, a model of careful work. It contains a notable bibliography of Bantu linguistics on pages 204-221.

It is possible that in the future Luba will play an increasingly important part among the Native languages of the Belgian Congo. Professor E. de Jonghe in an article in 'Congo' in 1933 entitled <u>Les Langues Communes au Congo Belge</u> examined the language situation there. He enumerated the four most important languages imposed over large areas of the Congo as (ki)Swahili, (li)Ngala, (tshi)Luba and (ki)Kongo. He pointed out that under European influence Swahili, in its local (ki)Ngwana form had been degraded to 'un vulgaire sabir'; that similarly Kongo had been degraded to the speech called 'Fiote'; that Ngala, in its 'Bangala' form, does not merit the name of literary language; while Luba, called 'Baluba', was the least deformed of all. He emphasised that each of the four languages had a host of dialectal variants and each required standardisation and unification. De Jonghe then pointed out the great advantage of one official Native language for the whole colony, and after discussing the merits and handicaps of each, unhesitatingly voted that Luba should be so recognised and developed. De Jonghe has urged this thesis in other publications (e.g. 'Semaine Missiologie Louvain' 1933, and the Bull. Inst.R.Colon.Belge' 1935), and has received considerable support, e.g. by Ch. Badoux in 'Outre Mer', 1936.

(o) <u>Luunda</u>: Spoken in the Katanga district of the Belgian Congo. This must be rigidly differentiated from Lunda, belonging to the West-central zone. No dictionary or vocabulary work[1] is known on this language, which presents (as evidenced from the New Testament translated by T.B. Brinton and others) the strange phonetic phenomenon of final vowel clipping, unknown elsewhere in Bantu.

(c) <u>Kanyoka</u>: Spoken to the north of the Luunda and the west of the Luba, between the Lubilashi and the Bushimaie Rivers between 6°.50 and 9° South latitude. Our information upon this language[2] comes from several publications by Mgr. A. de Clercq. In 1900 he published his Eléments de la langue Kanioka,[3] and in the next year a <u>Vocabulaire Kanioka-français</u>[4] and a <u>Vocabulaire français-Kanioka</u>. Modern tendencies have been towards the encouragement and development of Luba and the dropping of scientific work upon Kanyoka.

(d) <u>Nkoya</u> and <u>Mbwera</u> are both spoken in the western areas of Northern Rhodesia, to the east of the Upper Zambesi. Apart from New Testament translation and a MS. vocabulary of Nkoya, we have nothing yet upon which to work on these two languages.

---

1 Apart from what appeared in 'Koelle' in 1854.
2 Apart from one of Koelle's vocabularies entitled 'Kanyika'.
3 pp.44.
4 Vanves, 1901, pp.91.

(2) Bemba Group.

(a) Bemba, the chief cluster in the group, is spoken in North-eastern Rhodesia, north and east of Lake Bangueolo. Last included a vocabulary in his 'Polyglotta', and H.H. Johnston two vocabularies (one of 'Ki-wemba' and one of 'Ki-emba') in his 'British Central Africa' of 1897. In 1900 J.D. published an Essai de Grammaire Kibemba of 60 pages.[1] W. Govan Robertson of the London Missionary Society wrote An Introductory Handbook to the Language of the Bemba-People (Awemba) published in 1904. This book[2] contained 100 pages of grammatical notes, followed by a 'Bemba-English Vocabulary' (pp.103-404) and an 'English-Bemba Vocabulary' (pp.407-545). The book has long been out of print. It was compiled at Kawimbe near Abercorn from materials supplied from Bemba slaves and immigrants among the Mambwe and includes a Mambwe bias. More purely Bemba is Father Schoeffer's Grammar of the Bemba Language, which was edited by J.H.W. Sheane and arranged with a preface by the scholar A.C.Madan. This little outline was published by the Oxford University Press in 1907.[3] W. Lammond produced his Lessons in Bemba[4] in 1916; this useful little graded study of 100 lessons reached a second revised edition, entitled Lessons in Chibemba[5], in 1923. It was based on Schoeffer's Grammar. In 1920 L. Guillerme published his Dictionnaire français-Kibemba, a work of considerable size, and about this time the Union Bemba Language Committee issued a 'Vocabulary'. In 1921 E.B.H. Goodall put out his well-known little vocabulary Some Wemba Words, which has been widely used. In 1926 Lammond produced his Bemba-English Vocabulary, under the auspices of the Union Bemba Language Committee. This has proved a valuable little book (of some 300 pages) in which the semantic differences of vowel length were appreciated and recorded. A scientific study of the phonetics of Bemba was made by B.H.Barnes and C.M. Doke during 1929, and the results published in a paper entitled The Pronunciation of the Bemba Language, in 'B.St.' (Vol.III, No.4, pp.423-456). This was illustrated by kymograph and palatograph records and embodied certain proposals regarding orthography. Mention might be made of Fox-Pitt's little Chibemba Note Book containing lists of English-Bemba words and blanks for further recording. W.G.Robertson left a MS. of a Bemba-English Dictionary[6], and the White Fathers have a large dictionary in process

---

1 I have not seen a copy of this, published by Belin Frères, Saint Cloud; pp.xv, vii, 391.
2 pp.xxii + 545.
3 pp.72.
4 pp.122.
5 pp.160.
6 To be found in the South African Public Library, Cape Town.

of publication.[1] In 1935 E. Noël published Elements de Grammaire Kibemba.

Vocabularies of both Mambwe and Lungu dialects appear in Johnston's 'British Central Africa', while the former is exemplified in D. Picton Jones' Outlines of Ki-mambwe Grammar[2] with appended vocabularies, published as early as 1893.[3]

The more distant dialect of Tabwa, spoken west and south-west of Lake Tanganyika to the region of the Lualaba River, has been exemplified particularly by two writers. G. de Beerst was the author of an Essai de Grammaire Tabwa which appeared in the 'Z.A.O.S.'[4] in 1896. This constitutes a very good outline of the grammatical structure well exemplified. In 1907 in the 'Annales du Musée du Congo' was published A. van Acker's Dictionnaire Kitabwa-Français et Français-Kitabwa, a large-sheet double-column work of 170 pages, a useful vocabulary of the language.

(b) Aushi, spoken along the Luapula River, has been little investigated linguistically. Emil Birkeli used it in a small comparative study of 'Bausi, Malagasy, Bisa and Lala'[5]. In this are some vocabulary lists and a study of roots. C.M. Doke published A Short Aushi Vocabulary[6] in 1933 to fill in the blank left in H.H. Johnston's 'Comparative Vocabularies'.

(c) Lamba is spoken mainly in the Ndola district of Northern Rhodesia and the southern Katanga district of the Congo Belge. Reference may be made to an article entitled Lamba Literature published in 'Africa'[7] in 1934 by C.M. Doke, for a survey of this language. The first grammatical analysis was made by A.C. Madan in his Lala-Lamba Handbook[8] in 1908. This was however mainly Lala. In 1920 H.J. Collard published a Petite Grammaire du Lala-Lamba, tel qu'il se parle de Sakania à Elisabethville. Pure Lamba grammar was treated in C.M. Doke's Grammar of the Lamba Language[9] of 1922, in which however an

---

1 Burssens refers to a Dictionnaire Kibemba-français of the Missions Salésiennes, La Kafubu, Katanga (Cf. 'Schets van het Tshiluba', p.210); this, I understand, was published in 1929. I have also heard of a Petit Dictionnaire Kibemba-français, possibly from the same source. I have seen neither of these items.
2 pp.124.
3 A separate 'Vocabulary' of 64 pages was published in 1902.
4 II, 3, pp.271-287, and II, 4, pp.291-383.
5 I have a typed original of this unpublished French work of 42 pages.
6 'B.St.', Vol.VII, No.3, pp.285-295.
7 Vol.VII, No.3, pp.351-370.
8 pp.142.
9 pp.157.

ultra-disjunctive method of word-division was followed and old systems of classification and declensions used. The whole grammatical system was recast and rewritten with copious illustrations and appeared as a Text Book of Lamba Grammar[1] in 1938.   This work followed the system of the author's 'Text Book of Zulu Grammar';   it included a full phonological treatment, the semantic distinction of vowel lengths, a chapter on the ideophone and detailed syntax.   A chapter[2] to a large extent outlining this treatment had appeared in Doke's 'The Lambas of Northern Rhodesia' in 1931. The phonetics of the language had also previously appeared in a paper entitled A Study in Lamba Phonetics in 'B.St.'[3] in 1927.   In this scientific analysis a distinction had been made between 'normal grammatical phonetics' and the 'extra-normal phonetics' of onomatopoeic and emotional speech. In the field of lexicography Madan published a vocabulary of 65 pages (double col.) in his 'Handbook' already referred to, and in 1913 his Lala-Lamba-Wisa and English, English and Lala-Lamba-Wisa Dictionary of over 300 pages double-column. In this is an indiscriminate mingling of words from all three cluster representatives. This has proved of little practical value.   In 1933 C.M. Doke published an English-Lamba Vocabulary[4] of about seven thousand words, and in 1937 completed a large Lamba-English Dictionary[5] containing about 18,000 entries fully illustrated with idiomatic sentences.

No work has been done in the dialects of Lamba.

(d) Bisa, to the east of Lake Bangueolo, has been exemplified in the vocabularies of Last, Stanley and Johnston, and in the records of A.C. Madan, Wisa Handbook[6], with 83 pages of grammatical notes and word lists followed by an 'English-Wisa Vocabulary' of some 50 pages double column, published in 1906; and the 'Lala-Lamba-Wisa' dictionary, referred to above, and published in 1913. Birkeli also has reference to Bisa in the MS. referred to under Aushi, above.

(e) Of Lala, spoken south of Lake Bangueolo, the only records we have are those already referred to under Lamba., viz. Madan's Lala-Lamba Handbook, and 'Lala-Lamba-Wisa' Dictionary, as well as Birkeli's MS. on 'Bausi, Malagasy, Bisa and Lala'. This language is closely akin to Lamba.

---

1   pp. viii + 484 (replika).
2   'Language', Ch. xxiii, pp.367-386.
3   Vol.III, No.1, pp.5-47.
4   pp.134 (double col.).
5   This has not been published, six typed copies of 1957 pages being in existence.   One is in the British Museum Library.
6   Oxford: pp.136;   the initial consonant of 'Bisa', as of 'Bemba' is bi-labial fricative (phon.υ), variously interpreted as b, v or w.

(f) No special scientific records have been made upon Namwanga, spoken on the Nyasa-Tanganyika plateau.

(g) On Fipa, near Namwanga, we have B. Struck's Vocabulary of the Fipa Language[1], contributed to the 'J.A.S' in 1908.

(3) Tonga Group.

(a) Tonga (lang.ciTonga), sometimes referred to as 'Tonga of the Middle Zambesi', is spoken in the territory to the north of the Zambesi River from the region of Sesheke in the west to the Kafue River in the east. This language was first recorded by David Livingstone in a MS. vocabulary in the Grey Library at Cape Town; he referred to it by its Tswana pronunciation as 'Batoka'. It was Father J. Torrend, however, who made the language known, when he used it as his base of comparison in his well-known 'Comparative Grammar of the South African Bantu Languages' in 1891. His information at that time was obtained from three Natives brought to the 'Colony'. It was not until very much later in his career that Torrend came to reside among the Tonga and resume work in the language. Meanwhile, apart from some manuscript work done by officials and missionaries, in 1915 A.W. Griffin had produced his handy little Chitonga Vocabulary of the Zambesi Valley[2]. There are two recognised dialects of Tonga, Northern or 'Plateau' and Southern or 'Valley'. There is little difference between them. In 1918 appeared J.R. Fell's Tonga Grammar[3], a simple, orderly exposition following the principles of Smith's 'Ila'. A. Casset, S.J. produced, soon after this, his little Citonga Grammar and Vocabulary[4] 'for the use of the settlers between Livingstone and the Kafue', a little book of elements. Torrend re-entered publication in this group by issuing in 1930 a revised and enlarged edition of the Chikuni Mission Phrase Book in English and Citonga[5], under the title of An English-Tonga Phrasebook for Rhodesia[6], and in 1931 An English-Vernacular Dictionary of the Bantu-Botatwe Dialects of Northern Rhodesia[7], designed to serve the whole Tonga group (including Ila and Mukuni). Torrend was an important member of a committee seeking for a common literary language for the area; he was attracted by the 'definite numeral' construction in these languages typified by bantu botatwe for 'three people'.

---

1 pp.xi
2 pp.159. (Note on Nouns & Verbs pp.7-15; English-Chitonga, pp.27-99; Chitonga-English, pp.101-159.)
3 pp.130.
4 pp.171, of which 75 small pages dealt with grammar, and the rest was an English-Citonga Vocabulary.
5 1915; pp.38.
6 pp.122.
7 pp.xi + 649.

This fanciful term has not caught on. Torrend's dictionary is a valuable piece of work, and in it his sources of information and locality of terms are painstakingly recorded. Two other works of his must be recorded here. In 1932 appeared in rough mission printing from Chikuni his Nkanga Grammar ka Citonga[1], a very elementary Tonga grammar in the vernacular, being mainly a listing of words. In the same year Torrend issued, in mimeographed form, A Grammar of the Rhodesian Tonga[2] being 'introductory to the English-Vernacular Dictionary of Bantu-Botatwe and supplementary to "A Comparative Grammar of the South African Bantu Languages".' In this he ventilated certain strange theses concerning the 'natural order' of the noun classes and the importance of dividing nouns into the two groups of 'common' and 'proper'. While there is much valuable information in this work, it is marred by Torrend's fanciful interpretations. In 1940, C.R. Hopgood published Tonga Grammar, a Practical Introduction to the Study of Citonga[3], one of the most helpful books that have yet been prepared for the practical study of a Bantu language. It is based upon sentence drill and substitution table work, and formal grammar is only to be found scattered here and there. Constant reference is made to Ila and Mukuni variants, and also differentiation between Northern and Southern Tonga forms.

(b) Ila is spoken to the north of the Tonga country. For our scientific knowledge of Ila, the language of the Baila or Mashukulumbwe, as they are sometimes known by outsiders, we are almost entirely indebted to E.W. Smith. Coming to the country with a heritage of Sotho, Smith produced the first grammatical study in 1907, his Handbook of the Ila Language[4]. He introduced disjunctive writing[5], and set a grammatical form which was used by his colleagues. This book is a sound piece of work particularly noticeable, perhaps, for its full treatment of the 'Copula'. Grammar, with exercises and some reading material, occupies the first 254 pages; this is followed by 'English-Ila' and 'Ila-English' vocabularies. A popular little book Ila Made Easy[6] followed this in 1914, and in the same year an Ila Phrase Book of 48 pages; while Smith included a very able chapter[7] on 'The Ila Language' in Volume II of 'The Ila-Speaking Peoples of Northern Rhodesia'[8], published in 1920. E.W.Smith's contribution

---

1 pp.98.
2 pp.xii + 143; mimeographed from Torrend's handwriting; the work has never been published, but the author sent me a copy.
3 pp.xi + 235.
4 pp.xii + 488.
5 In later work Smith adopted a high degree of conjunctive writing.
6 pp.96.
7 Chapter XXVI (Vol.II, pp.277-310.)
8 By E.W. Smith and A.M. Dale.

is of no mean order. A scientific study of the phonetics was made by C.M. Doke in 1928 in a paper, An Outline of Ila Phonetics, contributed to 'B.St.'. This contained certain recommendations regarding orthography, as well as notes on Twa, Lundwe and Tonga.

(c) Mukuni, or Lenje, spoken between the Kafue and Broken Hill, is the third important member of this group. The only scientific study on this language is A.C. Madan's little Lenje Handbook[1] published by the Oxford Press in 1908. This is compiled in the style of all Madan's Central African Handbooks, with a short outline of grammar followed by vocabularies. Further vocabulary information may be obtained from Torrend's 'Bantu-Botatwe' Dictionary. Of the Twa language, spoken in the swamps of the Kafue and Lukanga, no study has yet been made.

(4) Zambesi Group.

Of the languages of this group, spoken along the Zambesi principally upstream from the area of the Victoria Falls (Luyi being found in Barotseland), first mention was made by Livingstone who compiled MS. vocabularies of Subiya and Luyi as early as 1851. We have no records of Leya. It was E. Jacottet, however, who provided the only detailed study of the group, when he published in 1896 Etudes sur les Langues du Haut-Zambèze[2] in three parts. The first part 'Grammaires Soubiya et Louyi' gives a straightforward exposition of the main grammatical elements treating first of Subiya then of Luyi. The second part consists of 'Textes Soubiya' and the third of 'Textes Louyi', followed by a short Luyi-French vocabulary. Jacottet had worked with Natives from the Zambesi who were in Basutoland, and his results reflect considerable credit on his linguistic ability. Luyi is the old 'Rotse' language which is now almost extinct. This language is also dealt with in the Comparative Vocabulary of Sikololo-Silui-Simbundu of A.W. Thomas and D.E.C. Stirke, published in 1916.

[5] EASTERN ZONE

Position: Generally speaking the languages of this zone cover Tanganyika Territory and the Northern section of Mozambique.

Characteristics: The main distinguishing characteristics of this zone are:

(i) A relatively simple phonology.

---

1 pp.154, grammar occupying pp.8-72.
2 Part I, pp.xxxvii + 133; Part II, pp.x + 181, Part III, pp.x + 238.

(ii) A three-tone system.
(iii) A simplification of verbal forms.
(iv) Locative formation tending to be intermediate between prefixal and suffixal.

Classification of languages: The following tentative grouping is based mainly on the arrangement followed by H.H.Johnston in his 'Comparative Study of the Bantu and Semi-Bantu Languages' (cf. Vol.II, pp.2-4).

(1) Nyamwezi, with dialects: Sukuma, Sumbwa, Nyaturu, Galaganza, Konongo, etc.

(2) Lacustrine group: (a) Kuria.
(b) Kwaya.

(3) Iramba.

(4) North-eastern group: (a) Pokomo.
(b) Taita, with dials. Dabida, Sagala.
(c) Taveta.
(d) 'Nika', with dials. Giryama, Duruma, Digo.

(5) Kilimanjaro group: (a) Chaga, with dials. Moshi, Siha, Meru.
(b) Pare, with dial. Asu.

(6) Shambala group: (a) Shambala, with dial. Bondei.
(b) Zigula.

(7) East-central group: (a) Zaramo, with dials. Kami, Ruguru.
(b) Sagara, with main dial. Kaguru.
(c) Gogo.
(d) Irangi.

(8) Rufiji group: (a) Hehe.
(b) Pogoro.
(c) Sango.
(d) Bena.
(e) Matumbi.

(9) Makonde, with dial. Maviha; allied Mwera, Ndonde.

(10) Sutu, with dial. Matengo; allied Pangwa.

(11) Kinga.

Insufficient is yet known concerning the inter-relationships of all these languages to make any classification certain. There are, further, numbers of other languages and dialects of which only short vocabularies or merely their names are as yet recorded.

(1) Nyamwezi: Spoken in the district of Unyamwezi in Tanganyika Territory extending southward from Lake Victoria, and embracing a

number of dialects,[1] the chief of which are Sukuma and Sumbwa.[2]

The earliest study of Nyamwezi which we have, is E. Steere's Collections for a Handbook of the Nyamwezi Language as spoken at Unyanyembe.[3] This little book, published in 1882, contains a grammatical outline, each part of speech being followed by a lengthy word list. It was of considerable value to pioneer workers. Last's vocabularies, of 1885, contained entries for Nyamwezi, and for Sukuma, Sumbwa and Galaganza. In 1898 A. Seidel contributed his Grundriss des Kinyamwezi[4] as an appendix to C.W.Werther's book, 'Die mittleren Hochländer des nördlichen Deutsch-Ostafrika'. C. Velten's Grammatik des Kinyamŭesi of 1901 was for long the best-known grammatical outline on the language. Dealing more especially with the Nyanyembe dialect, Velten followed 72 pages of grammar with a few pages of exercises and then devoted pages 88-302 to Nyamwezi-German and German-Nyamwezi vocabularies. In 1904 E. Dahl contributed a useful article, Die Töne und Akzente im Kiñamwezi, to the 'M.S.O.S'[5]. In the same journal in the same year, C. Meinhof contributed sections III, Namwezi[6] and IV, Sukuma[7] to his 'Linguistische Studien in Ost-Afrika'. In 1906 appeared R.Stern's Eine Kinyamwezi-grammatik, as an article in Volume IX of the above 'Mitteilungen'.[8] Of the total of 130 pages nearly 80 are devoted to classified lists of nouns and verbs. There is nothing original in the small amount of grammatical information vouchsafed. The work is based upon the Konongo[9] dialect. In 1915 E. Dahl produced his large Nyamwesi-Wörterbuch, which was

---

1 See B. Struck's article on the distribution of the Nyamwezi dialects in the 'Mitt.aus den Deutschen Schutzgebieten', 1910: Aus dem deutsch-ostafrikanischen Schutzgebiete - Begleitworte zur Dialektkarte von Unjamwesi, pp.101-110.
2 Johnston divides Nyamwezi as follows:
   (a) Typical Nyamwezi of N. and N-E: Sukuma-Rwana.
   (b) N-W. Nyamwezi: Sumbwa.
   (c) W. Nyamwezi: Galanganza (or Garaganja), Vinza, Bende, Gala.
   (d) S. Central and E. Nyamwezi: Nyanyembe, Konongo, and perhaps Shimbu and Nankwila.
3 pp.100.
4 pp.456-489; in which a brief grammatical outline is followed by some textual material with Swahili and German correspondences, and short vocabularies.
5 Vol.VII, pp.106-126.
6 Idem. pp.201-258.
7 Idem. pp.259-262.
8 Vol.IX, pp.129-258.
9 A. Capus is also credited with a Grammar of the Wakonongo Language. I have not seen this.

published as Vol.XXV. of the 'A.Hamb.K.I.'. This is an important work. The 'Nyamwesi-Deutsch' occupies pp.1-342 (double column), and the 'Deutsch-Nyamwesi' pp.345-696.

For Sukuma, A. Seidel gave a grammatical sketch and vocabularies in his Das Sukuma[1], published in 1894, which deals with the north-eastern dialects. Another account of the language was given by Captain C. Herrmann in his Kissukuma, contributed to the 'M.S.O.S.'[2] in 1898. This contained a grammar, with lists of words, tales, proverbs and songs with interlinear translation. The dialect dealt with was that of the north-western tribes, near Smith Sound and Speke Gulf. A much more scientific study of the language was made by J. Augustiny in his Laut- und Formenlehre der Sukuma-Sprache which appeared in 1929 in Vol.XXXII of the 'M.S.O.S.'[3]. The phonological part of this dissertation was based on the Meinhof system.

For Sumbwa we have the works of A. Capus, his 1898 Grammaire de Shi-sumbwa in the 'Z.A.O.S.', Vol.IV[4], and his Dictionnaire Shisumbwa-français[5] published in 1901. The grammar shews no originality, has the verb tenses set out in full in monotonous repetition, and treats as usual of 'le verbe être' and 'le verbe avoir'.

For Nyaturu there is W. Schregel's brief grammatical survey, Abriss einer Grammatik der Kinyaturu-Sprache printed in the 'M.S.O.S.'[6] in 1913. The only vocabulary as yet is the slight one given by Last.

(2) The Lacustrine Group:

Two languages of this group spoken on the eastern shore of Lake Victoria have been illustrated by A. Sillery in his Sketch of the Kikwaya Language[7] in 1932, and his Notes for a Grammar of the Kuria Language[8] in 1936. These are but outlines of languages spoken by small populations, Kwaya being spoken by about 21,000 souls and Kuria by some 65,000. Short specimens of Kuria, Ikoma, Jita, Nguruimi and Zanake were supplied by Miss A. Werner in 1927 in Specimens of East African Bantu Dialects[9]. In 1914 O. Dempwolff had published in

---

1 pp.18.
2 Vol.I, pp.146-198.
3 Vol.XXXII, pp.146-198.
4 pp.1-96 and 97-123.
5 pp.147.
6 Vol.XVI, pp.60-92.
7 'B.St.', Vol.VI, pp.273-307, comprising grammatical outline, folk-tales and vocabulary.
8 'B.St.', Vol.X, pp.9-29.
9 'B.St.', Vol.III, pp.1-3.

the 'Z.f.K.S.' under the series title of 'Beiträge zur Kenntnis der Sprachen in Deutsch-Ostafrika', his phonetic analysis of Kulia, following Meinhof's method of comparison with Ur-Bantu. This included a short grammatical analysis of the language also.[1]

(3) Iramba: Spoken to the north of the central railway in Tanganyika, and practically in the centre of that territory. Dempwolff included Ilamba as No.5 in his series Beiträge zur Kenntnis der Sprachen in Deutsch-Ostafrika, giving the phonology and grammatical outline according to Meinhof's method.[2] A somewhat similar treatment, comparing the language closely with Ur-Bantu, was given in 1922 by E. Ittameier in his article Abriss einer Lautlehre und Grammatik des Kinilāmba contributed to the 'Z.E.S.'[3] In 1925 F. Johnson contributed Notes on Kiniramba[4] to the journal 'B.St.'. This was but a short grammatical outline. This was followed in the same year by a Kiniramba-English and English-Kiniramba Vocabulary.[5] In 1942 G.N. Anderson, in his Tentative Studies in Ilamba Grammar and Phonetics (cyclostyled)[6] contributed further to our knowledge of the language.

(4) North-Eastern Group:

(a) Pokomo, spoken on both banks of the Lower Tana, behind the coast belt. Very little has been done in this language. In 1850 Krapf supplied a limited vocabulary in his Vocabulary of Six East African languages. In 1889-90 F. Würtz published two articles in the 'Z.A.S.', Zur Grammatik des Kipokomo (pp.161-189), and Kipokomo-Wörterverzeichnis (pp.81-106); and in 1895 his Wörterbuch des Ki-Tikuu und des Ki-Pokomo was published posthumously in the 'Z.A.O.S.'[7] In this the German entries were followed by the Tikulu and Pokomo equivalents.[8] In

---

1 Vol.V; phonology, pp.26-44; grammar, pp.113-136.
2 'Z.f.K.S.', Vol.V, pp.227-253.
3 Vol.XIII, pp.1-47.
4 'B.St.', Vol.II, pp.167-192.
5 'B.St.', Vol.II, pp.233-263.
6 pp.55 + 14 (foolscap).
7 Vol.I, pt.iii, pp.194-230; pt.iv, pp.289-313; reprinted as a separate volume in the same year, pp.63.
8 In the 'Strange Collection of Africana' (Johannesburg Public Library), is an interesting manuscript vocabulary prepared by F.Würtz and bearing date 'Lamu, 30.11.1892'. It is entitled Vocabularium in Deutsch-Kiunguya, Kiamu, Kitikuu, & Kipokomo, I. This comprises some 94 foolscap pages and beautifully-penned Arabic-script Swahili equivalents are included. This is the first folio of the MS. from which Seidel did his editing, taking out only the Tikulu and Pokomo material.

the following year Würtz's Grammatik des Pokomo was published in Vol.II of the same journal.[1] In 1905 Meinhof included in his 'Linguistische Studien in Ostafrika'[2],No.VII dealing with Pokomo, treating of it with his usual comparative method.[3]

(b) Taita, spoken in the Taita Hills south of Ukambani and east of Kilimanjaro, was one of the four languages dealt with by A. Downes Shaw in his Pocket Vocabulary of East African Languages in 1885. In 1894 J.A. Wray published An Elementary Introduction to the Taita Language in which he gave a useful outline of the grammar of the 'Sagalla dialect' followed by an 'English-Sagalla Vocabulary'.[4] A Vocabulary of French-Swahili-Taita[5] was published by Father Héméry at Zanzibar in 1901, while another short vocabulary of Taita by H.R. Tate appeared in the 'Journal of the Anthropological Institute' in 1904. H. W. Woodward contributed in 1913 Kitaita or Kisighau, 'as spoken on the Shambala hills above Bwiti' to the 'Z.f.K.S.'[6] This was but a very short grammatical outline.

(c) Taveta, south-east of Kilimanjaro, is only illustrated by Johnston's vocabulary in his 'Kilimanjaro Expedition' of 1886.

(d) 'Nika', used as a linguistic term by Krapf and Rebmann[7], indicates such languages as Giryama, Duruma and Digo. These were first illustrated by Ewald as early as 1846 in the 'Z.D.M.G.'[8], by Krapf in 1850 in his Vocabulary of Six East African Languages, and in his Outline of the Elements of the Kisuáheli Language in which there is frequent reference to 'Nika'. E. New published a Nika Vocabulary[9] in 1873; and in 1885 Shaw included it in his Pocket Vocabulary of East African Languages. Fuller treatment was given in A Nika-English Dictionary[10] by L.Krapf and J.Rebmann, which after many years delay was eventually edited by T.H. Sparshott and published in 1887. This is a dictionary of no mean proportions, and reflects very considerable research on the part of those pioneers. The nouns were arranged on the old principles of prefix instead of stems. Taylor[11] charac-

---

1 Pt.i, pp.62-79; pt. ii, pp.168-194.
2 'M.S.O.S.'; Vol.VIII, pp.201-222.
3 Rowling and Wilson in their 'Bibliography of African Christian Literature' (1923) refer to a Ki-Pokomo Grammar and Dictionary (Pokomo-Swahili-German) of the Neukirchener Missionsanstalt.
4 Grammar, pp.5-76; Vocabulary, pp.77-128.
5 I have not seen a copy of this, which is referred to by Johnston.
6 Band IV, Heft 2, pp.91-117.
7 Cf. 'Bantu Pioneers', p.242.
8 Vol.I, p.44.
9 I have not seen a copy of this.
10 pp.vii + 391 (double col.).
11 African Aphorisms, p.144.

terises this work as 'invaluable as a "thesaurus" of genuine native idioms'. Languages of this area were treated by Meinhof in 1905 in his 'Linguistische Studien in Ostafrika'[1], No.V Digo, and No.VI Nika, when the phonology and grammatical elements were compared to his hypothetical Ur-Bantu. In 1887 W.E. Taylor produced a Giryama Vocabulary, and in 1891 his Giryama Vocabulary and Collections[2], which contains a few grammatical notes, mainly concerning the verb, and certain other interesting material. Most recently Florence I. Deed has produced (cyclostyled) a book of Giryama Exercises, designed for beginners in the language. This comprises 85 quarto pages, including keys to the exercises.

(5) Kilimanjaro Group:

(a) Chaga, the most important member of this group, with various dialects, Moshi, Siha, Meru, etc., is spoken on the flanks of Kilimanjaro from north-east to north-west and on the Arusha Plain. Valuable information on this area was given by H.H. Johnston in 'The Languages of the Kilimanjaro District', Chapter XX of his 'Kilimanjaro Expedition'[3], 1885. In 1895 A. Seidel contributed a few pages, Uebersicht der grammatischen Elemente des Ki-chagga[4], as also did K.Walther to the same journal[5] in 1900, in his Beiträge zur Kenntniss des Moshi-Dialekts des Ki-Chagga. In 1905 H.A. Fokken contributed Das Kisiha[6], a phonological study, on the Meinhof pattern, of one of the principal dialects of Chaga. But the outstanding source of information on Chaga was produced in 1909 by J. Raum, when he wrote Versuch einer Grammatik der Dschaggasprache (Moschi-Dialekt)[7]. This monograph, published as Vol.XI of the 'A.Stud.D.K.S.' deals comprehensively not only with the phonology, grammar and syntax of the language, but adds considerable textual material with German translation. It contains a mass of information.

(b) Pare and its dialects are spoken south-east of Kilimanjaro. The Gweno dialect was illustrated by Johnston in his 'Kilimanjaro Expedition' (1885) referred to above. In 1909 E. Kotz wrote his Grammatik des Chasu[8], published as Vol.X of the 'A.Stud.D.K.S.'; this is a short grammatical sketch of the Asu dialect of Pare, and the only work of any consequence on this cluster of languages.

---

1 'M.S.O.S.', Band VIII, Digo, pp.177-185, Nika, pp.186-200.
2 pp.xxvii, 140.
3 pp.478-500 deal with the Bantu languages, Chaga, Gweno and Taveta: and pp.521-534 with vocabularies of the same.
4 In the 'Z.A.O.S.', I, iii, pp.231-238.
5 Vol.5, pp.28-43.
6 'M.S.O.S.' VIII, pp.44-85.
7 pp.399.
8 pp.vii + 79.

(6) Shambala Group:

(a) Shambala is spoken in the mountainous country of the Usambara district of Tanganyika. In 1867 E. Steere published his little Collections for a Handbook of the Shambala Language[1] comprising a grammatical note and certain word lists. A second edition[2] revised by H.W. Woodward appeared in 1905. In 1895 A. Seidel contributed to the 'Z.A.O.S.'[3] a study on the language entitled Beiträge zur Kenntnis der Shambalasprache in Usambara. This formed the basis of his monograph publication of the same year, entitled Handbuch der Shambala-Sprache in Usambara, Deutsch-Ostafrika[4], which contained a grammatical analysis of 55 pages, followed by textual material and vocabularies. In 1900 appeared a book which seems to have been very little known, M.E. Hörner's Kleine Leitfaden zur Erlernung des Kishambala[5]. This is a fairly comprehensive graded study with numerous exercises and vocabulary lists. In 1904 Meinhof dealt with Shambala in his series, 'Linguistische Studien in Ostafrika', II Sambala[6], giving a full phonological analysis. In 1906 Alice Werner contributed Notes on the Shambala Language to the 'J.A.S.'[7]. Karl Roehl published in 1911 a very important treatise on the language, Versuch einer systematischen Grammatik der Schambalasprache.[8] Great attention is given in this to the subject of tone. It contains, further, one of the most detailed treatments of the noun classes given in any Bantu grammar, no less than 86 pages being devoted to this subject; certain aspects of the verb, too, are worked out with meticulous detail.

In 1912 a Schambala-Grammatik by Frau Missionar O. Rösler and a Wörterbuch by Franz Gleiss were published as Vol. XIII[9] of the 'A.Stud.D.K.S.'. The grammar is of a very elementary type with exercises, and the vocabularies are very limited. In 1921 as Vol. XXXIII of the 'A.Hamb.K.I.' was published F. LangHeinrich's Schambala-

---

1 pp.vii + 81.
2 pp.vii + 72.
3 Vol.I, i, pp.34-82; ii, pp.105-117.
4 pp.135.
5 pp.340. Alice Werner has the following entry: 'P. Erasmus Hörner, Grammatik der Shambalasprache, Mariannhill, Natal, 1899. This is not in the catalogue of the British Museum Reading Room'.('J.A.S.', Vol.V, p.158). Possibly she is referring to this 1900 publication.
6 'M.S.O.S.', Vol.VII, pp.217-236.
7 Vol.V (No.XVIII), pp.154-166.
8 Vol.II of the publications of the Hamburg Kolonialinstitut; pp.xvi + 215.
9 pp. x + 134; grammar pp.1-52; 'Schambala-Deutsch', pp.54-101; Deutsch-Schambala, pp.102-134.

Wörterbuch[1], a large and informative dictionary of considerable value. F. Gleiss was the author of a little Schambala Sprachführer.

Bondei, the principal dialectal form of Shambala, is spoken in the lowlands between the Usambara Mountains and the coastal strip. In 1882 H.W. Woodward made a valuable contribution to our knowledge of East African Languages with his Collections for a Handbook of the Boondéi Language[2], copying this modest title from his superior, Bishop Steere's, Nyamwezi study. In this, after 56 pages of grammatical notes, fairly comprehensive 'English-Boondéi' and 'Boondéi-English' vocabularies are given. Last included the language in his Polyglotta Africana Orientalis of 1885. G. Dale produced Bondei Exercises[3] in 1892. In 1906 Meinhof included Bondei as No.VIII in his 'Linguistische Studien in Ostafrika'.[4]

(b) Zigula, spoken to the north of the Usambara Mountains, was illustrated first in H.M. Stanley's 'Through the Dark Continent' in 1878, and in Last's Polyglotta Africana Orientalis of 1885, where there was also a vocabulary of the Nguru dialect. Woodward also published 'a small collection of words' at about this time. About 1896 W.H. Kisbey produced his useful little book Zigula Exercises[5], which had a second edition in 1906. This contained a considerable amount of grammatical material. In 1902 Archdeacon Woodward published Collections for a Handbook of the Zigula Language[6], a much smaller work than his book on Bondei bearing a similar title. In 1906 Kisbey produced his Zigula-English and English-Zigula Dictionary[7], a little book of considerable practical value. In the same year Meinhof gave his phonological analysis of the language in No.IX of his 'Linguistische Studien in Ostafrika'.[8]

(7) East-central Group: Zaramo is spoken in the angle of the Kingani River and the coast of Tanganyika Territory, north of the Rufiji River; while westwards of this in turn are found the Kami, the Kaguru and the Gogo, and to the north of the last the Irangi.

(a) Zaramo: The earliest record we have of this language is the little collection of words and phrases published in 1869 by E.Steere

---

1 pp.502 (double col.).
2 pp.xvi + 236.
3 pp.102, with over 200 errata corrections.
4 'M.S.O.S.' Vol.IX, pp.278-284.
5 pp.116.
6 pp.61; this had been preceded by a little 15-page Kizigula-English Vocabulary in 1896.
7 pp.120.
8 'M.S.O.S.', Vol.IX, pp.284-293.

in his Short Specimens of the Vocabularies of Three Unpublished African Languages[1]. These were 'Gindo, Zaramo and Angazidja'. The 'Z.A.O.S.' published three papers on this language; in 1897 A.Worms' Grundzüge der Grammatik des Kizaramo[2], and Maass and Seidel's Beiträge zur Kenntnis des Kizaramo[3], and in 1898 Worms' Wörterverzeichnis der Sprache von Uzaramo.[4] Meinhof reviewed these works and gave a resume of the features of this language in the 'M.S.O.S.'[5] in 1907. Dempwolff also dealt with a phonetic phenomenon of Zaramo in his short article Eine lautliche Sonderheit des Dzalamo[6] in 1912.

The Kami dialect was illustrated by Last in his 1885 Polyglotta Africana Orientalis, and by A. Seidel in his Beiträge zur Kenntniss des Ki-Kami in Deutsch-Ostafrika, contributed to Z.A.O.S.[7] in 1896, but our main source of information on Kami is C.Velten's Kikami, die Sprache der Wakami in Deutsch-Ostafrika[8]. This was Velten's doctor's thesis presented in 1899. It was published in Vol.III of the 'M.S.O.S.' in 1900, though it had appeared in separate form the previous year. Containing only 27 pages of grammatical material followed by 29 pages of phrases and vocabulary, this seems a very weak effort for a doctor's thesis.

The Ruguru dialect was illustrated in 1898 by A. Seidel's contribution of a Grundriss der Wa-Ruguru-Sprache[9], as an Appendix to C.W. Werther's 'Die mittleren Hochländer des nördlichen Deutsch Ost-Afrika'. The grammatical sketch is followed by textual material with Swahili correspondences and German translation and very short vocabularies.

(b) Sagara may be used as the general term for a group of closely allied dialects, spoken in Usagara, a hilly region in Tanganyika. According to H.H. Johnston the chief dialects are Kaguru, Itumba, Kondoa or Solwe, Ziraha, Kwenyi, Nkwifiya and Nkunda. All of these are briefly illustrated in Last's 'Polyglotta'. The northernmost and most important dialect, Kaguru, is more fully exemplified in J.T. Last's Grammar of the Kaguru Language[10], a handy little grammatical and vocabulary study published in 1886. A short study of

---
1 pp.21.
2 Vol.iii, pp.289-310.
3 Vol.iii, pp.311-317.
4 Vol.iv, pp.339-365.
5 Vol.X, No.3, pp.90-110.
6 Contributed as part 2 of his 'Beiträge zur Kenntnis der Sprachen in Deutsch-Ostafrika', 'Z.f.K.S.', Vol.2, pp.257-260.
7 Jahrg, 2, pp.3-32.
8 pp.1-56.
9 pp.435-455.
10 pp.147; of which the first 90 pages treat of grammar, the remainder an 'English-Kaguru Vocabulary'.

Sagara and Gogo was included by H. Raddatz in his 'Die Suahili-Sprache'[1] in 1892.

(c) Gogo. Considerable attention in the field of Bible translation[2] has been given to this language, but little grammatical work has been published, and apart from travellers' vocabularies and those of Last, we have only G.J. Clark's Vocabulary of the Chigogo Language[3] of 1877, and O.T. Cordell's little Gogo Grammar, Exercises, etc.[4], printed in great difficulties at Mpwapwa in 1941.

(d) Irangi. Last included a short vocabulary in his 'Polyglotta' (1885). A. Seidel contributed a grammar and vocabulary in an appendix to C.W. Werther's 'Die mittleren Hochländer des nördlichen Deutsch Ost-Afrika' of 1898. This was entitled Grammatik der Sprache von Irangi[5]. Fifteen quarto pages of grammatical notes were followed by a few pages of textual material with Swahili correspondences and German translation, and vocabularies, also with Swahili correspondences. In 1915 O. Dempwolff published as No.8 of his 'Beiträge zur Kenntnis der Sprachen in Deutsch-Ostafrika'[6] a phonetic and short grammatical study of Irangi.

(8) Rufiji Group: Spoken south of the previous 'East-central Group' and in the vicinity of the Rufiji River.

(a) Hehe, spoken in the hill-country between the Ruaha and Ulanga Rivers, was included in Last's 'Polyglotta' (1885). In 1899 C. Velten contributed to the 'M.S.O.S.'[7] his paper Die Sprache der Wahehe. This contained a short grammar, a collection of phrases, stories (with interlinear Swahili and German translation) and a vocabulary. In 1900, in the same journal[8], appeared Kihehe-Wörter-Sammlung, by C. Spiss. This is a useful vocabulary of the language. In 1911 O. Dempwolff made Das Verbum im Hehe[9] the first study in his series 'Beiträge zur Kenntnis der Sprachen in Deutsch-Ostafrika'; this is a sound study upon a phonetic basis.

(b) Pogoro, spoken to the south-east of Uhehe in the Ulanga valley. The only published work on this language which we have is P.J. Hendle's

---

1 'Einige Dialekte aus dem Innern', pp.59-65.
2 The New Testament (in 1899) and numerous O.T. books have appeared.
3 pp.58.
4 pp.117.
5 pp.387-434.
6 'Z.f.K.S.' Vol.VI, pp.102-123.
7 Vol.II, pp.164-241.
8 Vol.III, pp.114-190.
9 'Z.f.K.S.', Vol.II, pp.83-107.

Die Sprache der Wapogoro[1], a short grammatical study followed by 'Deutsch-Chipogoro' and 'Chipogoro-Deutsch' vocabularies. This appeared in 1907.

(c) <u>Sango</u>, spoken south-west of Uhehe, though a language of considerable importance, has been little illustrated. Under the name of 'Rori' a fragmentary vocabulary was given by Stanley in Vol.ii of 'Through the Dark Continent', and Last also illustrated it in his 'Polyglotta'. It was however chosen by Meinhof as one of the types of Bantu analysed phonetically in his <u>Grundriss einer Lautlehre der Bantusprachen</u>[2] in 1899. This language is deserving of fuller grammatical treatment than it has hitherto received.

(d) <u>Bena</u>. The only information we have on this language is from the short vocabulary in Last's 'Polyglotta' (1885), and R.von Sowa's <u>Skizze der Grammatik des Ki-Bena (Ki-Hehe) in Deutsch-Ostafrika</u>, in 'Z.A.O.S.'[3] for 1900.

(e) <u>Matumbi</u> has been described by Bernhard Krumm in two contributions to the 'M.S.O.S.'. In 1912 he published <u>Grundriss einer Grammatik des Kimatumbi</u>[4], a short survey of the grammar followed by some pages of texts. In 1913 came his <u>Kimatumbi-Wörterverzeichnis</u>[5], a considerable German-Matumbi and Matumbi-German vocabulary.

(9) <u>Makonde</u>: Spoken in the coastal regions of Tanganyika and Northern Mozambique behind the Swahili coastal settlements. It was first illustrated by Steere in his <u>Collections for a Handbook of the Makonde Language</u>[6] which was printed at Zanzibar in 1876. Last included a vocabulary in his 'Polyglotta'. There are also vocabularies of Makonde and its principal dialect, Maviha, in 'Apontamentos para o Estudo das Linguas falladas, etc. da Provincia Portugueza de Mocambique, etc.' by J. d'Almeida da Cunha, Vol.I published at Loanda in 1886. Johnston points out that some of the information contained in this transcript is derived (with acknowledgments) from the various papers by Consul H.E. O'Neill published on pp.403-4 in the 1883 volume of the 'Proceedings of the Royal Geographical Society'. In 1899 C. Schumann contributed <u>Grundriss einer Grammatik der Kondesprache</u>[7] to

---

1 Published as Vol.VI of the 'A.Stud.D.K.S.'; pp.vii + 171.
2 pp.132-148, or pp.196-212 of the 2nd edition 1910; the Sango study was omitted from the English version, <u>Bantu Phonology</u>.
3 Jahrg. 5, pp.63-75.
4 Vol.XV, pp.1-63.
5 Vol.XVI, pp.1-59.
6 I have not seen a copy of this; pp.58.
7 pp.86.

the 'M.S.O.S.' In 1914 A. Lorenz published his <u>Entwurf einer</u> Kimakonde-<u>Grammatik</u> in the 'M.S.O.S.'[1] This contained a grammatical outline, a short vocabulary and some Makonde tales. F. Johnson, in 1922, published in the 'B.S.O.S.' short <u>Notes on Kimakonde</u>[2]. These are of a very elementary character, with vocabularies. In the following year they were concluded with fifteen folk-tales.

<u>Maviha</u> was well illustrated by L. Harries in <u>An Outline of Maŵiha Grammar</u>[3] published in B.St. in 1940. This grammar has been prepared on modern principles and includes a treatment of ideophones. Harries refers to vocabularies of Maviha in publications by the following: Froberville (1846), Hale (1846), Bleek (1856), Livingstone (1874), Maples (1880), and O'Neill (1882-3).

Allied to Makonde are the <u>Mwera</u> and <u>Ndonde</u> languages. Of the former the only source of information is R. von Sowa's brief <u>Skizze der Grammatik des Ki-mwera in Deutsch-Ostafrika</u>, published in the 'Z.A.O.S.', Vol.II, 1896. Of the latter Johnston gives some information gleaned from a vocabulary drawn up by Archdeacon Woodward in 1916 under the name of 'Kimawanda'.

(10) <u>Sutu</u>: Spoken in Southern Tanganyika between the Upper Rufiji, on the north, and the Upper Rovuma, on the south. A fairly comprehensive vocabulary of the language is given in the 'M.S.O.S.' in 1904, where C. Spiss wrote a lengthy article entitled <u>Kingoni und Kisutu</u>[4]. The grammar preceding the vocabularies deals only with Ngoni, the dialect of Zulu as spoken in Tanganyika.

The <u>Matengo</u> dialect is illustrated by J. Häfliger's <u>Kimatengo-Wörterbuch</u> published in the same journal[5] in 1909.

The allied <u>Pangwa</u> language, spoken in the mountainous country north-east of Lake Nyasa, is illustrated only by a brief phonetic survey on the Meinhof principle by M. Klamroth in his <u>Kurze Skizze der Lautlehre des Kipangwa</u>, published in the 'M.S.O.S.'[6] in 1907.

(11) <u>Kinga</u>: Spoken in the Livingstone Mountains bordering the East Coast of the northern end of Lake Nyasa. Our source of information on this language is R. Wolff's <u>Grammatik der Kinga-Sprache</u>[7] published

---

1 Vol.XVII, pp.46-117.
2 Vol.II, Pt.III, pp.417-466; Vol.III, Pt.I, pp.1-32.
3 'B.St.', Vol.XIV, pp.91-146. Texts with English translation followed on pp.410-433.
4 Vol.VII, pp.270-414; the vocabularies German-Ngoni-Sutu occupy pp. 307-414.
5 'M.S.O.S.', Vol.XII, pp.131-214.
6 'M.S.O.S.', Vol.X, pp.183-192.
7 pp.viii + 243.

in 1905 as Vol.III of the 'A.Stud.D.K.S.'. This contains a thorough grammatical treatment (of 108 pages) followed by considerable textual material with translations, and vocabularies Kinga-German and German-Kinga.

[5a] NORTH-EASTERN ZONE

Position: Originally along the coast-line of Kenya, Tanganyika and on the islands, e.g. Zanzibar, Comoro, etc.; later influence stretched right across Kenya and Tanganyika to Uganda, the Congo Basin and Northern Rhodesia.

Characteristics: Those of the Eastern zone with a further simplification of morphology due to the heavy impregnation by Arabic.

Classification of languages: The main language in this zone is Swahili, but a classification may be made as follows:

(1) Swahili; with main dialects, Lamu, Mvita, Unguja and Ngwana.
(2) Tikulu.
(3) Komoro; with dials. Ngazija, Nzwani.

(1) Swahili.

Linguistic studies in Swahili have been mainly confined to the Mombasa (Mvita) and Zanzibar (Unguja) dialects, and the results have been published principally in English and German, though there are certain items in French and some even in Portuguese and Dutch.

L. Krapf's early Swahili Grammar and East African Vocabularies of 1850 have already been observed.[1] His great work, however, was <u>A Dictionary of the Suahili Language</u>[2], published in 1882, the year after the great scholar's death. Krapf brought his knowledge of Arabic to bear upon this work and, despite the disadvantages of the orthography he employed, it has remained to this day 'indispensable to every student of Swahili, and has the permanent value and charm of genuine philological pioneer work by an honest and able researcher. It deals almost entirely with the dialect of Swahili used at Mombasa, and revision might make it more practically useful by the removal of inaccuracies and repetitions, but such treatment would be analogous to re-writing Schliemann's Troy or Livingstone's Journals.'[3] The dictionary was re-edited[4], however, in 1925 by Canon H.K. Binns, who had worked in the country since 1876. Binns

---

1 'Bantu Pioneers', p.242-3.
2 pp.xl + 433, double col.
3 Preface to A.C. Madan's <u>Swahili-English Dictionary</u>, pp.iii, iv.
4 <u>Swahili-English Dictionary</u>, S.P.C.K., pp.301 (double col.).

revised the spelling and arrangement, and omitted Arabic and Latin references. Though he did not include any explanation of the orthography he used, his work does not deserve the severe censure of Canon Hellier who wrote, 'Unfortunately this dictionary was re-edited in 1925, and completely spoiled in the process, the student should therefore secure a copy of the original edition.'[1] But such a copy is not easy to secure today!

The pioneer worker in the Zanzibar dialect was Bishop E. Steere. As early as 1870 he published the first edition of A Handbook of the Swahili Language as spoken at Zanzibar[2]. The grammatical part of this work is brief and elementary. Copious English-Swahili vocabularies are included in the first part; and the second part consists of a Swahili-English vocabulary. A second edition appeared in 1875, a third in 1882, which third was revised by A.C. Madan and printed by the S.P.C.K. in 1884, a fourth in 1894, and numerous other editions since. This book was for long the grammatical text-book for English students of Swahili. Steere published another useful and popular little book, his Swahili Exercises[3], which has been of inestimable value in the training of missionaries and, since the Great War, of officials in the language. In 1902 Starr refers to editions of this as early as 1882 and 1886; I have not seen these. In 1929 the edition reached its eighteenth thousand, a short supplement was added in 1931, and in 1934 appeared an edition 'revised and partly re-written' by A.B. Hellier[4]. The book has been adopted by the Inter-territorial Language Committee 'as the standard grammar of the Swahili language, and as embodying the conclusions of the Committee itself'. It is a very useful little book, but obviously falls far short of being a 'standard grammar' as it is neither written as a classified grammar nor does it delve into many of the intricacies of the language.

In 1885 Shaw had included Swahili in his 'Pocket Vocabulary of East African Languages'. Much syntactical and grammatical information on the language was given by W.E. Taylor in his African Aphorisms or Saws from Swahili-land, which was published in 1891. Taylor recognised aspiration and other significant differences in Swahili in this valuable little treatise, which must be dealt with elsewhere. In this, as also in another publication The Groundwork of the Swahili Language[5] (1898), Taylor dealt with Mvita and with the poetical Ngozi form of Swahili. In 1890 appeared anonymously a little Phrase-book, Swahili-English[6], containing short vocabularies and a collection of dhow-searching questions; while in the next year C. Slack published his little 16-page Introduction to

---

1 Swahili Prose Literature, in 'B.St.' Vol.XIV, p.251.
2 pp.xvi + 232 (Part I) + 189 (Part II).
3 pp.viii + 118.
4 pp. xi + 159.
5 I have not seen this publication. The full title is The Groundwork of the Swahili Language, namely, the concords; tabulated, exemplified, and illustrated for the use of those learning Swahili in East Africa and elsewhere.
6 pp.68.

Swahili; for the use of travellers, students and others. In 1892 the Universities' Mission published A Practical Guide to the Use of the Arabic Alphabet in writing Swahili according to the Usage of the East Coast of Africa.[1]

A worthy successor to Bishop Steere in linguistic labours came with A.C. Madan, who laboured on Bible revision and on the supply of education literature[2]. In 1894 Madan published his well-known English-Swahili Dictionary[3], an admirable work dealing with the Zanzibar form. This has been of inestimable value for many years. A second edition appeared in 1902; while in 1903 appeared the companion volume, Swahili-English Dictionary[4]. This pair of books formed the basis of A Standard English-Swahili Dictionary and A Standard Swahili-English Dictionary, which were the result of long labour by the late Frederick Johnson and which were published after his death as official publications of the Inter-territorial Language Committee of the East African Dependencies, in 1939. These two volumes constitute a mine of lexicographical information upon Swahili, particularly of the Zanzibar type. In 1905 Madan had published a little Swahili (Zanzibar) Grammar[5], a forerunner of the series of little handbooks he wrote on Central Bantu languages; while in 1917 he issued an English-Swahili Vocabulary[6] useful as an index to Steere's 'Swahili Exercises'.

In 1910 A.C. Hollis contributed to the 'J.A.S.'[7] an interesting Vocabulary of English Words and Sentences,' translated into six Languages or Dialects, viz.:- Zanzibar Swahili (Ki-Unguja), Mombasa Swahili (Ki-Mvita), Lamu Swahili (Ki-Amu), Patta Swahili (Ki-Pate), Siyu Swahili (Ki-Siu) and Bajun (Faza) Swahili (Ki-Tikuu).' In 1910 also was issued Mrs. F. Burt's Swahili Grammar and Vocabulary[8], an attempt to adapt the Berlitz method to Swahili. W.E. Taylor furnished an introductory section dealing with the dialects and phonetics. Taylor's orthography was followed throughout. A second edition appeared in 1917 and several reprints since that date.

About 1915 appeared two books of very considerable merit in the study of Swahili linguistics. M.W.H. Beech was the author of Aids to the Study of Ki-Swahili[9], containing an exposition of Swahili (Arabic)

---

[1] pp.57.
[2] cf. Hellier's article Swahili Prose Literature, 'B.St.', Vol. XIV, p.252.
[3] pp.vii + 415 (double col.).
[4] pp.xix + 442 (double col.).
[5] pp.62.
[6] pp.56.
[7] Vol.X, pp.1-24; issued also as a 24-page reprint.
[8] Second edition reprinted 1923, pp.263.
[9] pp.xvi + 159; n.d., but probably published about 1914.

writing with numerous examples of letters, followed by stories with translation and notes on idiom, and other literary features, such as aphorisms and enigmas. Beech also had works on Borneo Dialects and the Suk to his credit. The other book was C.M.Stigand's A Grammar of Dialectic Changes in the Kiswahili Language[1] (1915), commonly referred to as 'Dialect in Swahili'. This contains a lot of valuable information illustrating change in sounds, in grammar, in vocabulary and in idiom. Taking Unguja as his standard, he compares in turn Mrima,Mgao,Hadimu and Tumbatu,Pemba, Mvita, Vumba, Lamu, Pate, Shela, Siu, Tikuu, the dialects of the Banadir Coast, Ngazija, and Ngovi or Ngozi. The book is also noteworthy for an appendix containing a recension and poetical translation of the poem 'Inkishafi' contributed by W.E. Taylor. The Hadimu dialect was further illustrated by Miss A. Werner in an article in the 'J.A.S.'[2] in 1916. W. H. Ingram's paper The Dialects of the Zanzibar Sultanate, contributed to the 'B.S.O.S.'[3] in 1924, contains short vocabularies of Unguja, Pemba, Tumbatu, Hadimu (with three sub-dialects), Pepo and Mundi, together with Ngazija (a Komoro dialect). There are also specimens of Ganga, the speech of the medicine men.

In 1926 Fathers A. Reichart and M. Küsters published in the series 'Gaspey-Otto-Sauer' an Elementary Kiswaheli Grammar[4] accompanied by a 'Key'[5] Little need be said of this: it is a very faulty publication, and the method does not lend itself to Bantu languages; it is written, too, in very poor English. In 1927 the sisters A. and M. Werner published a very useful First Swahili Book[6] based on a type of direct method. This little book is thoroughly reliable, and contains some useful idiomatic reading matter. A much more elementary book,appearing also in 1927, was G. Murray-Jardine's Abridged Swahili Grammar[7], containing phrases, stories and vocabulary. In 1929 the Education Department, Tanganyika, issued A Guide and Aid to Swahili Examinations, a little 74-page book designed for one practical purpose. In 1929 R.R. Scott published A Glossary of some Scientific Terms used in Sanitary Practice by Swahili-speaking Africans.[8] This is a very useful collection. In 1937 P.J. Greenway published at Dar-es-Salaam A Swahili Dictionary of Plant Names[9], a valuable piece of work. Miss M. Bazett was the author of Everyday Swahili Phrases and Vocabulary, published at Nairobi; and N. Victor, of the Universities' Mission,published The Essentials of Swahili, a series of grammatical tables.

1 pp.xi + 105 (of which pp.73-105 are an appendix contributed by Taylor).
2 The Wahadimu of Zanzibar, Vol.XV, pp.356-360.
3 Vol.III, pp.533-550.
4 pp.viii + 350.
5 pp.64.
6 pp.viii + 127.
7 pp.63.
8 pp.65.
9 pp.xvi, 112.

Two interesting articles contributed to 'Africa' by G.W. Broomfield might be noted here. They are The Development of the Swahili Language[1] in 1930, and The Re-Bantuization of the Swahili Language[2] in 1931. The latter is of considerable interest, and is a reply to K. Roehl's article The Linguistic Situation in East Africa[3], which appeared in 1930 in the same journal.

In 1932 B.J. Ratcliffe and H. Elphinstone produced their Modern Swahili[4], a book aimed at practical guidance in learning Swahili among the various forms found in the East African Territories. It contains exercises, specimen examination papers and vocabularies. The book contains certain fresh material, but it is questionable whether the method of presentation is any improvement on previous publications.

In 1933 the Inter-Territorial Language (Swahili) Committee to the East African Dependencies commenced printing their Bulletin with No.6. Previous numbers had been cyclostyled. There is some very valuable linguistic material in the form of memoranda and discussion in these Bulletins[5] which reached No.18 in 1944. In the later numbers attention has been drawn to the phenomenon of the ideophone in Swahili.

In 1935 Mrs. E.O. Ashton wrote a thought-provoking article on the study of Swahili, entitled The 'Idea' Approach to Swahili[6]. In the same year E.B. Haddon issued in typed cyclostyle his Notes on Swahili Grammar[7]. This was one of the best treatments of Swahili grammar up to that time. An attempt was made to bring the classification, treatment and terminology into line with what has been done for Zulu and other Bantu languages — an elimination of the non-Bantu approach. Haddon delved much more deeply into the intricacies of Swahili grammar than any previous writer.

In 1944, however, Mrs. Ashton brought out her Swahili Grammar (including intonation), a work of some 398 pages, graded for students and including numerous exercises. The work contains many innovations, such as drill in correct tone pronunciation — of characteristic and grammatical tone, for Swahili is a stranger to semantic tone. There are other interesting and provocative grammatical innovations, which certainly seem to assist the practical learning; but perhaps the greatest contribution of this book is the revelation that Swahili is not as deficient in Bantu grammatical intricacies as one has been led to believe from earlier grammars. For the comparative student it is unfortunate that the grammar is not arranged in blocks of study according to the various phenomena — its purpose has been that of a graded study. This is certainly the best thing

---

1 'Africa' Vol.III, pp.516-522.
2 'Africa' Vol.IV, pp.77-85.
3 'Africa' Vol.III, pp.191-202.
4 pp.xviii + 310. The book has been well commented upon by Krumm.
5 They vary in size from 10 pages to 30 pages.
6 In the 'B.S.O.S.' Vol.VII, pp.837-859.
7 pp.117, large quarto.

we have in Swahili.

Dr. A.N. Tucker and Mrs. E.O. Ashton published in 'African Studies'[1] in 1942 Swahili Phonetics, a fairly comprehensive survey of the subject, despite the impossibility, owing to war conditions, of using Arabic type.

       x   x   x

We now turn to the German contribution to Swahili linguistic studies. Several German writers, such as Krapf, Reichart and Küsters, had contributed through the medium of English. We now consider those who used German medium for their books.

The earliest monograph we have is C.G. Büttner's Hülfsbüchlein für.. Unterricht in der Suahili-Sprache[2] of 1887. Next is W. von St. Paul Illaire's Suaheli Handbuch[3], published in 1890 as the second volume of the series 'Lehrbücher des Seminars fur Orientalische Sprachen'. This is quite a comprehensive grammatical study, including an important section on Syntax. In 1890 Büttner, the eminent literary worker in Swahili, published his Wörterbuch der Suaheli-Sprache, Suaheli-Deutsch und Deutsch-Suaheli[4] as Volume III of the above series; and as Volume X of the same series his Suaheli-Schriftstücke[5], to which he added a valuable appendix discussing Arabic script and Swahili orthography. In 1892 also appeared H. Raddatz's Die Suahili-Sprache[6], in which was a short grammatical outline of 38 pages followed by phrases, a German-Swahili vocabulary of 47 pages and a Swahili-German vocabulary of 53 pages. Raddatz also included a short comparative study of the Sagara and Gogo languages and an appendix on Sudan Arabic. In 1891 was issued Dr. F. Freiherr von Gravenreuth's Suaheli-Dragoman[7], a practical guide to the language for use in 'Deutsch-Ostafrika'. In 1896 Illaire produced his Suaheli Sprachführer, a large volume of nearly 600 pages giving vocabulary, phrases and conversation covering a very wide range of subjects and topics (there are also eleven pages of errata!). In 1898 S. Domet, a Syrian Arab, wrote Die Suaheli-Sprache[8].

One who contributed considerably at about this time was A. Seidel who wrote Das arabische Element im Suaheli in 1895 in the 'Z.A.O.S.'[9]

---

1 Vol.I, pp.77–103, 161–182.
2 pp.96; 2nd edition 1891.
3 pp.xxvi + 202.
4 pp.ix + 269.
5 This is an important contribution to Swahili literature.
6 pp.xiv + 176. A second edition edited by A. Seidel was issued in 1900.
7 pp.xii + 256.
8 Published at Jerusalem. I have not seen a copy of this.
9 Vol.I, Pt.1, pp.9–15; Vol.I, Pt.2. pp.97–104.

and in the same journal Beiträge zur Kenntniss des Lamu Dialectes[1]. In 1900 Seidel published his Suahili Konversations-Grammatik[2] in the series 'Methode Gaspey-Otto-Sauer'. With this important work was issued a 95-page Schlüssel. He had preceded this by his Praktische Grammatik der Suaheli-Sprache[3], the first edition of which was in 1890. In 1902 Seidel published his Systematisches Wörterbuch der Suahilisprache[4], in which a very useful vocabulary of Swahili words is arranged according to an elaborate system of classified subjects.

In 1896 E. Ovir contributed Die abgeleiteten Verba im Kiswahili to the 'Z.A.O.S.'[5]. A Deutsch-suaheli Taschen-Wörterbuch[6] was put out in 1900 by O. von Baudissin. In 1904 C. Meinhof dealt with Swahili in No.1 of his 'Linguistische Studien in Ostafrika'[7]. This was a short general description of the sounds and Arabic influence thereupon. Meinhof further wrote a little book, Die Sprache der Suaheli in Deutsch-Ostafrika[8], as Vol.II of the series of 'Deutsche Kolonialsprachen' in 1910. The name of C. Velten is the next one of importance in Swahili linguistics. In 1901 he published his Praktische Anleitung zur Erlernung der Schrift der Suaheli[9]. In 1904 he produced his Praktische Suaheli-Grammatik[10], a fairly detailed grammar replete with examples and followed by a German-Swahili Vocabulary. This went through several editions, of which a second appeared in 1905, a third in 1910, a fourth in 1913 and a fifth in 1932. Velten's greatest contribution was in the subject of lexicography. In 1910 he produced Suaheli-Wörterbuch, I Teil, Suaheli-Deutsch[11], and in 1933 his bigger Suaheli-Wörterbuch, II Teil, Deutsch-Suaheli.[12] These two volumes are a real contribution and are comparable to the parallel English works of Madan, of whose books he was able to make use. Velten was also the author of a Taschen-Wörterbuch der Suaheli-Sprache[13] published in 1911, a very useful little publication. Besides his textual publications, which will be considered elsewhere, he produced in 1901 a Praktische Anleitung zur Erlernung der arabischen Schrift der Suaheli[14], and in 1910 Suaheli-Sprachführer für Postbeamte.

---

1 Z.A.O.S., 1895, Vol.I, Pt.2, pp.169-183.
2 pp.xvi + 404.
3 pp.viii + 182.
4 pp.xii + 178.
5 Vol.II, Pt.3, pp.249-266.
6 pp.142.
7 'M.S.O.S.' Vol.VII, pp.202-216.
8 pp.viii + 109.
9 pp.105.
10 pp.x + 308, of which 179-308 is the vocabulary.
11 pp.xv + 529 (double col.).
12 pp.xii + 883 (double col.).
13 Small, 8cm.x 11cm., pp.252 (double col.).
14 pp.105.

W. Planert wrote in 1907 Die syntaktischen Verhältnisse des Suaheli[1]. An article dealing with 'aspiration' was contributed in 1911 by the well-known experimental phonetician G. Panconcelli-Calzia to the 'Z.f.K.S.'[2], entitled Über die aspirierten Verschlusslaute sowie den Frageton im Suaheli. In 1923 H. Jensen contributed to the 'Z.f.E.S.' a short article, Ausgewählte Kapitel aus der Syntax des Suaheli[3]; and in 1929 M.Klingenheben-v. Tiling in the same journal[4] wrote Lautliche Eigentümlichkeiten im gesprochenen Suaheli. B. Krumm produced in 1932 Wörter und Wortformen orientalischen Ursprungs im Suaheli[5], a scientific examination of the eastern contribution to the make-up of Swahili, including not only classical Arabic, but also southern Arabic, Persian, Turkish and certain Indian languages. In 1940 the Sheldon Press published the English version of this book, Words of Oriental Origin in Swahili[6], enlarged and brought more up-to-date. This is a scholarly piece of work and examines and criticises all previous publications on the subject. A valuable glossary is added.

In 1939 Dr. K. Roehl edited a third edition of Siegfried Delius' 'Grammatik der Suaheli-Sprache', under the title of Wegweiser in die Suaheli-Sprache[7]. The first edition had been published in 1910, and the second in 1927.[8] This third edition constitutes a fine exposition of Swahili grammar with numerous reading lessons. An accompanying Wörterverzeichnis[9], comprising 2500 'Suaheli-Deutsch' and 2900 'Deutsch-Suaheli' words, was published separately.

x   x   x

French contributions to Swahili Studies are also not inconsiderable. The earliest I have seen is P. Dutrieux's Vocabulaire Français-Kisouahili[10], published by the Association Internationale Africaine in 1880, and containing only about 1800 words; but Père Daull's Grammaire de Kisouahili[11] is said to have been published at Colmar in 1879. St. Paul Illaire refers to a Manuel de Conversation en Kiswahili published in 1881 by the Fathers of the Congrégation du St. Esprit et du St.Coeur de Marie at Bagamoyo[12],

---

1 pp.59.
2 Vol.I, pp.305-315.
3 Vol.XIII, pp.241-260.
4 Vol.XX, pp.1-10.
5 pp.90.
6 pp.x, 192.
7 pp.x + 228.
8 Reprinted in 1936, pp.viii, 141; with a 'Schlüssel' and 'Wörterverzeichnis' as a separate publication, pp.60.
9 pp.86.
10 pp.112.
11 pp.125; entitled Grammaire Kisouahili in the New York Public Library catalogue.
12 I have not seen a copy of this.

and states that a lithographed Vocabulaire Français-Kiswahili et Kiswahili-Français was put out in 1885 from Algiers. Father Delaunay published his Grammaire Kiswahili[1] as early as 1885. It was subsequently republished and the edition before me is dated 1927.[2] This constitutes a fairly detailed account of the grammar, and devotes over 50 pages to a study of the syntax of the language. Delaunay published in the same year (1885) a Dictionnaire Français-Kiswahili, but I have not seen this. In 1891 C. Sacleux published his Dictionnaire français-swahili[3], a book of no inconsiderable size and merit. Sacleux was also the author of an extremely valuable dialectal study of Swahili, his Grammaire des Dialectes swahilis, which appeared in 1909. After a valuable introduction of 20 pages including a historical outline, he divided his book into three parts: (i) Phonétique (pp.1-38), (ii) Parties du Discours (pp.38-258), and (iii) Syntaxe, etc. (pp.259-332). Though the treatment is in the 'old style' there is much valuable information in this book. In the same year (1909) Sacleux published his Grammaire Swahilie[4], devoted to an extensive and detailed study of the Zanzibar dialect. Here, too, there is a great amount of valuable material. In 1894 the Etat Indépendant du Congo published a Vocabulaire Français-Kisouahili of 111 pages (interleaved with blank sheets). Commandant G. Moltedo of the Congo Free State issued a Petit Vocabulaire des Langues arabe et ki-swaili[5] in 1905. In 1911 appeared E. Brutel's Vocabulaire Français-Kiswahili et Kiswahili-Français, preceded by a grammatical outline. This was one of the publications of the Maison-Carrée press of the White Fathers. There is nothing particular to note about this publication, except that a second edition was called for immediately and a third in 1913.[6]

x   x   x

Of other language media we note the following. In 1890 in Gujerati script appeared Alidina Somjee Lilani's Guide to the Swahili Language in Gujerati characters, with English and Gujerati translations[7], chiefly for the use of Indians having relations with Zanzibar. In 1924 a vocabulary of Swahili appeared in the Portuguese publication of A.A.P. Cabral, Vocabulário Português, Shironga, Shitsua, Guitonga, Shishope, Shisena, Shinhungue, Shishuabo, Kikua, Shi-Yao e Kissuahili.[8] In 1926 Giacomo de Gregorio published in Italian at Palermo, Il Swahili nella Somalia italiana e i suoi elementi arabici. Flemish students in Belgian Congo are also interesting themselves in this language. O. Liesenborghs contributed in 1938 to 'Kongo-Overzee'[9] an interesting article entitled Wat is Kingwana?

---

1 pp.173; 2nd ed. was published in 1898.
2 pp.218.
3 pp.xix + 989; xxxvi + 4. I have not yet seen a copy of this.
4 pp.xvi, 268.
5 pp.31 + (17).
6 The 1928 impression of 2500 copies has 470 pages, of which the first 60 deal with grammar.
7 pp.204 +4.
8 pp.89.
9 Vol.IV, pp.233-249.

discussing the western dialect of Swahili. P. Colle also produced <u>Inleiding tot de Samenspraak in de Swahilische Taal, voorafgegaan door een korten inhoud der Swahilische Spraakleer</u>. A second edition was edited by E.P. Tielemans.[1]

x   x   x

More interesting however are the Swahili vernacular linguistic studies, which should in the future be more and more developed. In 1883 appeared an anonymous grammatical study of the language entitled <u>Sarufi ya Kiswahili</u>[2], while Madan produced as a 16-page pamphlet <u>Maelezo ya Sarufi ya Kiswahili</u> in 1888. Canon Broomfield published a similar study in 1931 under the same title[3] a most serviceable Swahili grammar for Swahili schools. He has demonstrated the possibility of a Swahili (Bantu) terminology for grammar based on bantuizations of the accepted English (or Latin) terms where applicable. In 1935 Frederick Johnson published a most valuable vernacular dictionary: <u>Kamusi ya Kiswahili yaani Kitabu cha Maneno ya Kiswahili</u>[4]. This is a veritable milestone in Bantu lexicographical studies. Swahili is the only Bantu language yet to have a vernacular dictionary, perhaps because it serves some ten million speakers. Johnson's book is good, but it can only claim to be an explainer of meanings, in no way does it touch upon constructional use or etymology. It is noteworthy that each of these vernacular contributions is written by a European — surely it is time the Swahili themselves entered this field!

Swahili does not lack exponents of its 'Kitchen' form. In 1936 F.H. Le Breton published what he termed <u>Up-country Swahili Exercises</u> 'for the soldier, settler, miner, merchant and their wives'.[5] His claim is that 'Correct Swahili is a very complicated language native to Zanzibar and the coastal belt of East Africa. To the ordinary up-country native, Swahili is a foreign language, of which he possesses only a very limited knowledge'. The author has indicated the true Swahili forms in italics in many cases, but his exposition of 'Up-country Swahili' reveals a language dispensing to a great degree with concord — 'in Up-country Swahili this is reduced to a minimum, the form used, being almost invariably that which agrees with the singular of the so-called N-class'. To the grammar and exercises are appended considerable vocabularies.

(2) <u>Tikulu</u>, closely allied to Swahili, is spoken in Faza on the coast north of Lamu and as far up as the Juba River. The Swahili call the language <u>Ki-Tikuu</u>. F. Würtz prepared a <u>Wörterbuch des Ki-Tikuu und des Ki-Pokomo in Ost-Afrika</u>, which was edited after his death by A. Seidel and published

---

1 There is no date to this edition. I have not seen a copy.
2 I have not seen a copy of this.
3 <u>Sarufi ya Kiswahili</u>, pp.xiv + 175.
4 pp.xvii + 261 (double col.).
5 Other editions 1937, 1940, 1941, the last consisting of 96 pages.

in 1895 in the 'Z.A.O.S.'[1] Reference may also be made to Hollis' 1910 Vocabulary, referred to under Swahili.

(3) Komoro, spoken on the Comoro Islands, between Zanzibar and Madagascar. Last published a short vocabulary of 'Anzuani of Hinzŭa' in his 'Polyglotta'; and vocabularies of the same dialect of Johanna Island were published by J.M. Hildebrandt in the 'Z.f.E.'[2] in 1876. Bishop Steere included in 1869 a short vocabulary of The Language of Great Comoro: Shiangazidja in his 'Short Specimens of the Vocabularies of Three Unpublished African Languages'[3]. In 1909 B. Struck contributed to the 'J.A.S.'[4], An Unpublished Vocabulary of the Comoro Language, from a manuscript entry in Guillain's historical work. He deduces that the entries were made by a French agent on Johanna Island, probably in 1856. The best analysis of Komoro however has been done by M. Heepe, who published, as his Doctor's thesis, in 1914, Die Komorendialekte Ngazidja und Nzwani[5]. In this he critically reviewed all previous references to and vocabularies of Komoro (Herbert 1626, Elliot 1821, Casalis 1841, Bleek—Peters 1856, Steere 1869, Gevrey 1876, Kersten 1871, Hildebrandt 1875, Last 1885, Torrend 1891, Struck 1909, and Sacleux 1909), and then gave a study of Ngazija and Nzwani phonology, a mere reference to grammatical forms, and a text with German translation. In 1920 Heepe published Die Komorendialekte Ngazidja, Nzwani, und Mwali[6], a work which incorporated the previous, but added a very considerable section of textual material, mainly in Ngazija.

[5b] EAST-CENTRAL ZONE

Position: Nyasaland and Northern Mozambique.

Characteristics: These languages constitute a bridging between those of the Central zone and those of the Eastern zone.

The most important languages of this sub-zone are:

(1) Nkonde.
(2) Nyasa group: (a) Tumbuka, with dials. Henga, Kamanga.
                 (b) Tonga.
(3) Western group: (a) Nyanja, with dials. Chewa, Mang'anja, Peta.
                   (b) Nsenga.
                   (c) Sena, with dials. Nyungwe, Chikunda, Barwe, Tonga.
(4) Yao, with dial. Ngindo.
(5) Makua: with Chwabo.

---

1 Reprinted in book form, pp.63, double col.
2 pp.89—96.
3 pp.18—21.
4 Vol.VIII, No.XXXII, July 1909, pp.412—421.
5 pp.vi + 55.
6 pp.xvi + 166, of which pp.51—166 are devoted to the texts.

(1) Nkonde, commonly referred to as 'Nyakyusa' is spoken in Tanganyika Territory to the north end of Lake Nyasa. One of the dialectal forms, 'Mwamba' was illustrated in a vocabulary[1] compiled by J.A. Bain and printed at Livingstonia in 1891. H.H. Johnston included a vocabulary of 'Iki-nyikinsa' in his 'British Central Africa'[2] in 1897. In 1899 C. Schumann contributed to the 'M.S.O.S.'[3] his Grundriss einer Grammatik der Konde-Sprache. While this work contains a fair amount of material, particularly in the vocabularies, it is very badly arranged and unsatisfactory to use for reference. In the following volume of the 'M.S.O.S.'[4] (1900) K. Endemann contributed a short discussion Zur Erklärung einer eigenthümlichen Verbalform im Konde. A detailed phonological exposition of the language appeared in C. Meinhof's 'Grundriss einer Lautlehre der Bantusprachen' (1899) in Chapter VIII,[5] headed Konde, the spelling of the name as used by German writers.

(2) Nyasa Group.

(a) The two main dialectal forms of Tumbuka, spoken on the west coast of the upper half of Lake Nyasa, are Henga and Kamanga. The former was illustrated by H.H. Johnston in his 'British Central Africa'[6] in 1897. In 1891 W.L. Elmslie had written Notes on the Tumbuka Language[7] and a Table of Concords, etc. of the Tumbuka Language. His 'Notes' was followed up with the Grammar of the Tumbuka Language[8], which has reached a fourth edition. D.R. MacKenzie published Notes on Tumbuka Syntax in 1911.[9] In 1923 appeared T. Cullen Young's Notes on the Speech and History of the Tumbuka-Henga Peoples[10]. In this book a study of language is combined with that of the history of the people, an unsuitable combination, as Dr. Westermann suggested in a review. In 1932 Cullen Young issued these two parts separately — Notes on the Speech of the Tumbuka-Kamanga Peoples[11] — and Notes on the History of the Tumbuka-Kamanga Peoples — with changed tribal title, a third volume, Notes on the Customs and Folk-lore of the Tumbuka-Kamanga Peoples, the third in the trilogy, having appeared in 1931. The grammatical notes could be greatly improved by re-arrangment and more up-to-date treatment.

(b) Tonga is spoken on the western shore of the central part of Lake Nyasa. The language is called 'chiTonga'. Johnston includes a

---

1 I have not seen a copy of this.
2 pp.496-503.
3 Vol.II, pp.1-86.
4 Vol.III, pp.93-95.
5 pp.110-131.
6 pp.504-513 of 3rd edition.
7 pp.32.
8 ? date.
9 or thereabouts, ? date. See Cullen Young's preface for these references.
10 pp.viii + 223.
11 pp.181.

vocabulary of this language in his 'British Central Africa'[1] of 1897.

(3) Western Group.

(a) Nyanja commonly called 'Chinyanja' is the unified standardised literary form used for government and educational purposes particularly in Southern Nyasaland. Contributing to this language have been particularly Mang'anja, Chewa and Peta. A closely allied form, differing somewhat dialectically, is the Nyanja spoken on the east coast of the Lake from the mission centre on Likoma Island.

Peta, the south-western form, also called Maravi, was probably first illustrated, under the name of Marawi, in Koelle's 'Polyglotta Africana'; it was also included in Bleek's 'Languages of Mosambique' in 1856. This is also the speech of John Rebmann's Dictionary of the Kiniassa Language[2] which was compiled during the years 1853 to 1855, but not published till 1877 when it had been edited by his colleague L.Krapf. This dictionary is a painstaking piece of work, shewing very considerable scholarship. It was, however, the result of research with a single slave from Mombasa, and suffers from that drawback. Nevertheless it is a model of what a scholar can do with such slender and unpromising material. A vocabulary of 'Ci-nyanja (Ci-cipeta)' is included by H.H. Johnston in his 'British Central Africa'[3] (1897).

Chewa, also illustrated by Johnston[4], is spoken on the south-west coast of the Lake, and extending into Northern Rhodesia. In 1937 M.H. Watkins produced a most creditable Grammar of Chichewa[5] based on a study of 'Some 400 pages of text with grammatical material, and more than 700 pages of ethnological description in English which include many expressions in the Native language. All the information was obtained from Kamuzu Banda, a Native Chewa, while he was in attendance at the University of Chicago, from 1930 to 1932'. The morphology, which occupies the bulk of the book, is treated on sound principles, and the author has managed to get away from the outworn European classificatory methods of so many writers of Bantu grammars. The whole book is uncommon in its method of treatment and definitely stimulating to any student of Bantu.

Mang'anja, the south-eastern form, was probably first illustrated by Alexander Riddel of the Livingstonia Mission in A Grammar of the Chinyanja Language[6] in 1880, a little book of grammatical notes and vocabularies. In 1891 Dr. George Henry of the same mission brought out a Grammar of Chinyanja, a much fuller treatment with exercises; these works

---

1 pp.504-513 of the 3rd edition.
2 pp.viii + 184 (double col.)
3 pp.514-520, of the 3rd edition.
4 ibid. pp.504-511.
5 pp.158.
6 pp.150.
7 A second edition was published in 1904(pp.viii+232), Dr. Henry having died in 1893 before accomplishing a revision he had in view.

helped to fix the name of the written language. In 1894 R. Laws produced at Edinburgh <u>An English-Nyanja Dictionary</u>[1]; he had previously (1885) produced his <u>Table of Concords and Paradigm of Verb of the Chinyanja language</u>. About the same time, probably, appeared the mission-printed <u>First Mang'anja Lessons</u>[2], and in 1896-7 a diminutive <u>Mang'anja Grammar</u>[3], with folding tables, also printed at the Blantyre Mission Press. About 1897 R. Caldwell dealt with Mang'anja in his <u>Chi-nyanja Simplified</u>, a little book which later reached a second edition[4] with a key to the exercises. In 1902 the Mission Press published <u>Mang'anja Unit of Thought</u>[5], a little booklet with vocabulary and model sentences. <u>Grammar and Exercises in Chi-mang'anja</u>[6], a little lesson-book in the vernacular was issued in 1917. Mang'anja, however, is best known from the monumental work of D.C. Scott, <u>A Cyclopaedic Dictionary of the Mang'anja Language</u>[7], which was published in 1892. The special feature of this dictionary was the inclusion of a great deal of ethnographic information upon words and customs recorded. Numerous idiomatic sentences and aphorisms illustrate the entries. Scott made a most valuable contribution in this cyclopaedic emphasis in his book, which is only marred by what have come to be called 'Scottisms' (Chi-Scott) in his choice and inclusion of derivatives. A revised and enlarged edition of this work was published in 1929 under the editorship of Alexander Hetherwick. This was entitled <u>Dictionary of the Nyanja Language</u>[8]. In this much of the ethnographic material was omitted and many new entries included to make it applicable to the form of Union Nyanja used in Nyasaland. This is a very useful book.

Of <u>Eastern Nyanja</u> we have the works of Miss M.E. Woodward who published in 1898 her <u>Chi-nyanja Exercise Book</u>[9], which served a very useful purpose. In 1892 she had been mainly responsible for a <u>Vocabulary of English-Chinyanja and Chinyanja-English as spoken at Likoma</u>[10]. Working upon that as a basis B.H. Barnes published in 1902 a very creditable <u>Nyanja-English Vocabulary</u>[11], and in 1913 an <u>English-Nyanja Vocabulary.</u>[12]

The grammar, however, which has become the standard for many years in Nyanja, is Alexander Hetherwick's <u>A Practical Manual of the Nyanja</u>

---

1 I have not seen a copy of this; pp.xi + 231.
2 Some 22 pages quarto, abt. 1894.
3 pp.24 + tables.
4 pp.88 + 46, in 1915.
5 pp.38 and folding table.
6 pp.28.
7 pp.682 (double col.) with English vocabulary appended.
8 pp.vii+ 612 (double col.). The English-Nyanja vocabulary was also omitted.
9 pp.vi+83; revised by B.H. Barnes in 1909 under title of <u>Nyanja Exercise Book</u>.
10 pp.67; 2nd ed. 1895.
11 pp.viii+183, with tables; revised and enlarged by M.W. Bulley in 1929.
12 pp.112, and folding table.

Language[1], the first edition of which appeared about 1904. Of this T. Price writes[2]: 'This work is eclectic in its selection of grammatical elements and vocabulary, but the dominant influence is that of Maŋanja, due to Dr. Hetherwick's long and unbroken residence in the Maŋanja country. The Nyanja, therefore, which the European learner picked up from books and tended to accept as standard was south-eastern, and broadly Maŋanja in type.' In 1915 the Zambesi Industrial Mission put out a very good English-Chinyanja Dictionary[3], which has proved of great practical value.

In 1925 appeared two grammatical studies: An Introduction to Chinyanja[4] by Meredith Sanderson and W.B. Bithrey, a work of very inferior calibre, and A Manual of Nyanja[5] by Miss M.W. Bulley, who really carried on the work commenced by Miss Woodward. Miss Bulley's 'Manual' is a practical work of considerable merit.

J.G. Steytler produced (2nd ed. 1937) Cinenedwe ca Cinyanja[6], a grammatical study in the vernacular, presented in an interesting and useful fashion.

The finest scientific study of Nyanja that has yet appeared is Emmi Meyer's Etymologische Lautlehre des Nyanja (Nyasaland), a doctor's thesis accepted by the 'Hansische Universität', and published in the 'Z.E.S.'[7] in 1936-1937. This is a very valuable phonetic study. Another valuable contribution to our knowledge of the position regarding literary Nyanja was furnished in 1940 by T. Price in his article, Nyanja Linguistic Problems, contributed to the journal 'Africa'[8]. This should be studied by all interested in Nyanja literature. Price followed this by publishing The Elements of Nyanja for English-speaking Students, in two parts, in 1941 and 1943[9]. Mrs. Ferreira has published in Afrikaans, Cinyanja Hulpboekie[10].

(b) Nsenga, spoken to the west of the Nyanja territory and throughout the whole eastern half of the valley of the Luangwa river in Northern Rhodesia, was very imperfectly illustrated by H.H. Johnston in his 'British Central Africa'. In 1905 A.C. Madan gave an outline of this language in his little Senga Handbook[11], largely composed of vocabularies. In

---

1 This has gone through several editions: 2nd ed. 1907, reprinted 1912, 4th ed. 1916 (pp.xx+ 299), 6th ed. 1922, 8th ed. 1932.
2 Cf. T. Price, Nyanja Linguistic Problems in 'Africa', Vol.xiii, No.2.
3 pp. xv + 381; a new edition appeared in 1940.
4 pp. 98.
5 pp. 76.
6 pp. 79.
7 Vol. 27, pp. 1-34, 129-155, 184-211.
8 Vol. XIII, No. 2, pp. 125-137.
9 Part I, pp. 1-129; Part II, pp. 130-304. I have not seen a copy of this.
10 I have no further information on this publication.
11 pp. 100.

1928, however, it was splendidly treated by A.S.B.Ranger in his Chinsenga Handbook[1], which besides a full exposition of the grammar, contains phrases, textual material and useful vocabularies. Though Ranger's work is definitely out-of-date in grammatical treatment, recording inter alia 'prepositions', 'verb to be', 'personal pronouns', it is a mine of information, replete with idiomatic examples and syntactical notes, his chapter on the Conjunction (of 28 pages) being especially good. This is a valuable book.

(c) The Sena group of languages is spoken along and in the vicinity of the lower Zambesi from about 100 miles upstream from its mouth to a distance of over 500 miles upstream. Of its position Johnston (using the dialectal term of Nyungwe) writes: 'Cinyuñgwi is spoken on both banks of the Lower Zambezi, west of the Ziwe-Ziwe confluence at Sena, especially at Tete and Sena, as far west as 32° of East longitude, where it grades into Cinseñga and Cinyai, and as far north as the Makañga country, the watershed of Lake Nyasa, where it grades into Maravi or Cipeta'. The three main dialects of this group are Sena, spoken in the vicinity of the town of that name, Nyungwe, often referred to as 'Tete' and spoken in the vicinity of the town of Tette, and Chikunda spoken still further upstream towards Zumbo. Vocabularies of the first two dialects appear in Bleek's Languages of Mosambique of 1856. Johnston gives a vocabulary of Nyungwe in his 'British Central Africa.'

For Sena, W.G. Anderson published in 1897 An Introductory Grammar of the Sena Language spoken on the Lower Zambesi[2], a very slight treatment. In 1900 J. Torrend published a small Grammatica do Chisena[3], a grammar of the language of the Lower Zambesi. Most of the material in this little grammar was arranged in three columns trilingually, Portuguese, Sena and English. In 1924 a much fuller treatment was provided by A. Moreira in his Practical Grammatical Notes of the Sena Language[4], published posthumously. This work contains nothing original in treatment, but gives a good picture of the language. A.A.P.Cabral included vocabularies of Sena and Nyungwe in his Vocabulário of 1924.

The most important worker in Nyungwe was V.J. Courtois, who, apart from much other vernacular work for the Mission at Boroma Monastery, published in 1899 his Diccionario Portuguez-Cafre-Tetense[5], a work embodying very considerable research and scholarship; it is a very full vocabulary with over 30,000 Portuguese entries with their Nyungwe equivalents. In 1900 Courtois published his Diccionario Cafre-Tetense-Portuguez[6], and in the same year his Elementos de grammatica tetense, lingua Chi-Nyungue[7].

1 pp.ix + 337.
2 pp.vi + 61.
3 pp.176.
4 pp.viii + 168, with a preface by F.P. Schebesta.
5 pp.xiii + 484, (double col.)
6 pp.xvii+81.
7 pp.xiii+ 231; this is described as a new edition; I do not know the date of the first one.

In 1904 A. Mohl published his Praktische Grammatik der Bantu-Sprache von Tete, einem Dialekt des Unter-Sambesi mit Varianten der Sena-Sprache und Woerterbuch[1]. This is in three sections, the first of which, dealing with grammar had appeared in fuller form earlier in the same year in the 'M.S.O.S.'[2]. The second part dealt with exercises and reading matter; the third consisted of vocabularies. In 1904 G. de Gregorio published in the Report of the 'Congrès International des Orientalistes' a study on the Nyungwe Language[3] by J.Torrend, but unauthorised by the writer[4]. In 1908 H. Simon produced a little poorly-roneod Resumo da Grammatica da Lingua-Chi-Nyungwe (Tete)[5], extracted, as he says, from the grammars of Dupeyron[6] and Torrend. In 1914 Torrend added to J. van Ginneken's article 'Les classes nominales des langues bantoues' in 'Anthropos', an appendix entitled La Liste complète de noms de la langue Nyungwe (Zambèze)[7].

No individual work has been done on the other dialects of this group.

(4) Yao is spoken in the uplands between the Rovuma and the Lujenda rivers, in Portuguese East Africa, whence it has spread into the Shire Highlands. H.H. Johnston records: 'A vocabulary of the Yao language, under the name of "Muntu", was given in Koelle's "Polyglotta Africana", and was attributed by him to the "Veiao". It represents the eastern form of the Yao language where it impinges on the Lomwe or Makua dialects, but is very near to the Nyasaland speech.'[8] Other vocabularies had appeared in collections earlier: Hale (1846), Krapf (1850), Koelle (1854) and Bleek (1856). Maples also published a Yao-English Vocabulary[9] at Zanzibar in 1888. In 1871 Steere published his Collections for a Handbook of the Yao Language[10]; and in 1889 appeared Hetherwick's Introductory Handbook and Vocabulary of the Yao Language. A second edition[11] of this, revised and enlarged, was issued in 1902. The major part of this useful little book is devoted to the vocabularies. In 1894 R.S. Hynde produced a Second Yao-English Primer of 104 pages. Soon after 1900[12] appeared Pedro Dupeyron's Pequeno Vademecum da Lingua Bantu na Provincia de Moçambique ou Breve Estudo da Lingua Chi-Yao ou Adjaua. This most interesting publication

1 pp.viii + 68 (1st part) + 108 (2nd & 3rd parts).
2 Vol.VII, Part iii, pp.32-85.
3 Etymologie des Soi-disant préfixes Dérivatifs des Langues Bantoues sur la base d'une étude spéciale sur le Chinyungwe, pp.147-171.
4 Cf. 'The Growth of Comparative Bantu Philology', 'African Studies', Vol.II, p.30.
5 56 small pages.
6 See Dupeyron's work under 'Yao', in which he deals also with Sena, Nyungwe and Chwabo.
7 Vol.IX, pp.781-800.
8 Comp. Study, Vol.I, p.794.
9 pp.114.
10 pp.vii + 105.
11 Entitled A Handbook of the Yao Language, pp.xxii + 420.
12 No date appears on the publication, but he quotes from Torrend's 1900 Sena publication, and is quoted by Simon in 1908.

contains a great amount of comparative material concerning Sena, Nyungwe and Chwabo, as well as the analysis and vocabulary of Yao. The first part (pp.1-40) is concerned with Yao grammar; the second (pp.41-116) deals with Yao compared with Sena, Nyungwe and Chwabo, the works of Torrend, Courtois and Desmaroux being cited, and gives a 'Breve Guia de Conversação' in Chwabo and Nyungwe; the third (pp.117-168) gives (i) a short vocabulary of Chwabo, and (ii) a much fuller 'Vocabulario Chyao-Portuguez'. Vocabularies of Yao appeared both in Last's 'Polyglotta' (1885) and in Johnston's 'British Central Africa' (1897). In 1908 Meinhof produced his phonological and grammatical study of Yao as No.XV of his series 'Linguistische Studien in Ostafrika' in the 'M.S.O.S.'[1]. In 1916 Meredith Sanderson published A Yao Grammar, which reached a second edition[2] in 1922. It contains some valuable information, but is not as reliable as Hetherwick's earlier work. In 1920 Sanderson published Notes on 'Chikala cha Wayao'[3] which had appeared the year before. These dealt with grammatical and constructional points. Cabral included Yao in his Vocabulário of 1924.

Of the Ngindo dialect we only have vocabularies by Last and Johnston.

(5) Makua is spoken in the Mozambique district of Portuguese East Africa; dialectal forms are Northern Makua or Medo and Western Makua or Lomwe; Chwabo, the language of Quelimane at the Zambesi mouth, is closely allied. Apart from the earlier vocabularies of Salt, Koelle and Bleek, short vocabularies of Makua and Lomwe appeared in the geographical papers of Consul H.E. O'Neill published in the 'Royal Geographical Society's Proceedings' in 1882 and 1884.

In 1879 Chauncy Maples published his little Collections for a Handbook of the Makua Language[4], dealing with the dialect spoken in the neighbourhood of Masasi. In 1886 D.J. Rankin published Arab Tales Translated from the Swahili Language into the Túgulu dialect of the Mákua Language: together with Comparative Vocabularies of Five Dialects of the Mákua Language.[5] The dialects dealt with were those of Maples, O'Neill and his own collection of 'Túgulu', together with 'Makónde' and 'Mbwabe'. In 1887 A. de Carvalho Soveral published a brief 31-page study, Breve estudo sobre a ilha de Moçambique acompanhado d'um pequeno vocabulario Portuguez-Macúa. Last included a vocabulary in his 'Polyglotta' and Johnston one of Southern Makua and one of Lomwe in his 'British Central Africa' in 1897. In 1901 A. Werner contributed to the 'J.A.S.'[6] A Vocabulary of the Lomwe Dialect of Makua (Mozambique), to which considerable comparative notes were added. During the years 1904-5 J.V. do Sacramento contributed to the 'Bol.Soc.de Geog. de Lisboa' a series, Apontamentos sobre a lingua

---

1 Vol.XI, pp.132-173.
2 pp.xii + 211.
3 pp.18.
4 pp.xii + 100.
5 pp.xv + 46.
6 Vol.I, pp.236-251.

macúa. About 1905 R.C.F. Maugham, H.B.M. Consul in Portuguese East Africa, produced A Handbook of the Chi-Makua Language[1], in which a most strange orthography is used 'primarily for the use of British searchers after knowledge', in which he uses 'the entire alphabet with the exception of the letter w'! The scientific study of the language came with Meinhof's phonological and grammatical exposition under No.XIV of his 'Linguistische Studien in Ostafrika', published in the 'M.S.O.S.'[2] in 1908. To this valuable exposition is added Meinhof's editing of the manuscript of the French-Makua Vocabulary of 1790 found in Berlin.[3] In 1926 H.W.Woodward contributed to 'B.St.'[4] An Outline of Makua Grammar. This was a very complete outline of the grammatical elements with short vocabularies and a folk-tale; other Makua Tales were published in a later number of the same journal.[5] Archdeacon Woodward left fairly full Makua-English and English-Imakuani Vocabularies in manuscript, which it is hoped will yet be published. Cabral included Makua in his Vocabulário of 1924.

Regarding Chwabo Dupeyron refers to a manuscript by Desmaroux, 'Grammatica inedita do E-Chwabo'. Much information on this language is to be gleaned from Torrend's Contes en Chwabo ou Langue de Quelimane, published in 1895-6 in the 'Z.A.O.S.'. Vocabularies were given by Almeida da Cunha in 1883 and by A.A.P. Cabral in 1924, the former in his Vocabularios das linguas da provincia de Moçambique[6], and the latter in his Vocabulário Português, Shironga, etc. etc.

[6] SOUTH-EASTERN ZONE

Position: Portuguese East Africa, the Union of South Africa, Bechuanaland and Basutoland, with isolated members beyond.

Characteristics:
(1) Both monosyllabic and disyllabic prefixes.
(2) Locative formation by suffix.
(3) Diminutive formation by suffix.
(4) Development of deficient verbs.
(5) Generally complicated tone system.
(6) Intricate phonology involving implosives, lateral fricatives, and in some cases clicks.
(7) Operation of phonetic laws of palatalisation and velarisation.

---

1 pp.39.
2 Vol.XI, pp.85-131.
3 Cf. 'Bantu Pioneers', p.212.
4 Vol.II, pp.269-325.
5 In March, 1932.
6 I, pp.9-56.

Classification of the languages:[1]

(1) Nguni group: (a) Zulu: dials. Zululand, Natal, Qwaɓe, Ndeɓele (Rhodesia), Ngoni (Nyasaland and Tanganyika).
                   (b) Xhosa: dials. Literary (Gcaleka and Gaika), Mpondo, Thembu, Mpondomisi, Bomvana.
                   (c) Swazi: dials. Swazi, Old Mfengu, Baca.

(2) Sotho group: (a) Northern: dials. Pedi, Kwena, Lovedu, Ndebele-Sotho, Masemola, Tlokwa.
                  (b) Southern (of Basutoland).
                  (c) Tswana: dials. Kgatla, Rolong, Tlaro, Tlaping, Ngwato, Tawana, Hurutsi, Kwena, Ngwaketse.
                  (d) Kololo (of Barotseland).

(3) Venda.

(4) Tsonga group (Shangana-Tonga):
                  (a) Ronga.
                  (b) Tonga: dials. Hlanganu, Jonga, Bila, Gwamba.
                  (c) Tswa: dials. Dzibi, Makwakwe, Hlengwe, Dzonga.

(5) Inhambane group: (a) Chopi (or Lenge).
                      (b) Tonga.

(1) **Nguni Group.** This group is divided into three cluster sections, each of which stands equally near to and equally distant from the other. Two of the groups, Zulu and Xhosa, are used as literary media. Swazi has not been so developed; but Ndeɓele, a dialect of Zulu, has been used to a certain extent for literary purposes.

(a) **Zulu.** Standard Zulu is today based on the Zululand form, with contributions from the Natal dialect. It is used throughout Zululand and Natal, the South-eastern Transvaal, and the Witwatersrand area. Dialectal forms are found in Ndeɓele in Matabeleland of Southern Rhodesia, in Transvaal Ndeɓele, and in Ngoni spoken in Nyasaland (particularly on the western side of the Lake) and in parts of southern Tanganyika.

For the earlier works in Zulu (pre-1860) reference should be made to 'Bantu Pioneers'[2], where J.C. Bryant, L. Grout, H.P.S. Schreuder, J. Perrin, J.L. Döhne and J.W. Colenso are more particularly dealt with. Colenso's *Zulu-English Dictionary*, dealt with there, first appeared in 1861 and later editions persist to the present day. Perrin's little *English-Zulu Dictionary* first published in 1855 is still in circulation. Another early voc-

---

1 For details of classification and literature concerning this zone, reference should be made to C.M. Doke, *A Preliminary Investigation into the State of the Native Languages of South Africa with Suggestions as to Research and the Development of Literature*, in 'B.St.' Vol. VII, 1933, pp. 1-98.
2 'B.St.', Vol. XIV, pp. 226-235.

abulary publication was Zulu Vocabulary and Phrase Book intended for the use of Immigrants and Settlers in the Colony of Natal, published without author's name by Cullingworth of Durban. This had a very large run of editions.[1] Another popular little book was S. Gibbs's An Easy Zulu Vocabulary and Phrase Book with Grammatical Notes first published in 1884. Other editions, published by Davis & Sons, Maritzburg, were in 1890[2], one with additions and amendments by R.C.A. Samuelson in 1903, and one issued in 1902 by the Central News Agency, Johannesburg as 'by a Zulu Interpreter and Translator', without author's name.

In 1880 Charles Roberts published the first edition of his well-known and much-used English-Zulu Dictionary. This was a solid piece of work containing the Zulu equivalents for about 10,000 English words. With the second edition in 1895 was added a supplement of some 400 additional words. Later editions were but fresh 'impressions'[3], the supplement not being incorporated in the body of the dictionary. In 1891 P. Mate published in German his Kleines Deutsch-Kaffrisches Wörterbuch[4], which illustrated Zulu. This embodies a fairly extensive treatment, but was of use almost exclusively to the Catholic missionaries of Mariannhill and other stations.

At about the same time A.T.Bryant issued Isigama, ukuti nje, Inncwadi yamazwi esingisi ecasiselwe ngokwabantu, under the pseudonym of 'uNemo'. Two impressions[5] of this appeared, undated, printed at Pinetown, Natal. This work doubtless acted as the basis for Bryant's Abridged English-Zulu Word-Book[6], which has had a very wide vogue both among English learners of Zulu and Zulu students of English. The 'Word-book' was issued at Mariannhill in 1917 and has been reprinted several times. Despite its wide use, it has several serious defects, chief of which is the lack of detailed differentiation in the meanings of English words. Students need constantly to cross-refer to the Zulu-English dictionary before being certain of using the right word. There are also a number of inaccuracies which Bryant should have avoided. Bryant's magnum opus, however, was his Zulu-English Dictionary[7] of 1915, which contained about 22,000 Zulu entries. This was a real advance on previous work in several directions. Words were arranged alphabetically according to stem, and verbal derivatives were reduced to those which had some special significance beyond the normal. What was most important was the inclusion of aids to pronunciation

---

1 I have not found the dates of the earlier editions, but the 4th was in 1873, the 5th in 1879, the 8th in 1892, the 12th in 1918 (pp.66).
2 pp.53.
3 e.g. 4th 1905, 5th 1911, 6th 1915.
4 pp.173 (double col.).
5 Each pp.249.
6 pp.467.
7 Now out of print; pp.778 (large) double col., with pp.111 of introductory matter.

indicating where aspiration existed and differentiating between explosive and implosive b. Of course these details will all be indicated naturally in a dictionary in the new Zulu orthography which makes provision for them. In a number of cases Bryant indicated intonation differences, though very inadequately. Large numbers of idiomatic and proverbial illustrations were included. The main criticisms against Bryant's handling are: (i) too rambling a method of explaining meanings, which could be more pithily stated, and (ii) the inclusion of numerous unnecessary and often fanciful comparisons with other languages, even far outside the Bantu area.

In 1923 R.C.A. Samuelson published his King Cetywayo Zulu Dictionary[1], which, though it added some new words, came nowhere near Bryant's standard, included numbers of unnecessary derivatives, and was guilty of numerous repetitions and missortings of words. In fact Samuelson's dictionary is a most annoying book with which to work. After giving 535 pages (double col.) from A to Z, he adds a repetition of another 30 pages of medical etc. terms, other special excerpts, 50 pages of 'Proverbs, Idioms and Useful Sayings'[2] (unfortunately in no order whatever), nearly 100 pages of excerpted words dealing with the Native Kraal and its occupants, and then 250 more pages (double col.) of an 'Extra Dictionary, being an extract from the General Dictionary of words and terms more commonly used'! Had he published merely the 535 pages of the general dictionary with the proverbs added in some order of reference, he would have made a vast improvement.

W. Wanger was responsible in 1913 for a specialized type of lexicon treated with true scientific acumen, his Catholic Zulu Terminology[3], as he states, 'an explanatory supplement to the Zulu Catechism by the same author.' The Catechism referred to is an enormous publication of over 500 pages, a scholarly piece of work, and the lexicon before us treats in detail of the words chosen in their theological setting. Even though some may dispute interpretations and meanings assigned to many words, the 'Terminology' is a valuable reference book. The words are arranged under the English, then German, Zulu and Latin indexes are added for cross-reference. From 1911 to 1913 Wanger had edited The Collector[4] composed of 944 paragraph sections of information culled from Native informants upon all types of ethnographic subjects. There is in this a great amount of valuable lexicographical material, in the handling of which Wanger has proved himself an adept. Another specialist vocabulary is provided in J. Gerstner's

---

1 pp. xliii + 995.
2 Though this is not acknowledged in the book, the proverbs were derived from a collection made by Mr. Carl Faye.
3 pp. 266.
4 iv + 1-20 (Apl.1911), vii + 19-48 (June 1911), xiv + 49-119 (Apl.1912), xiii + 121-183 including five pages dealing with Manyika of Southern Rhodesia (Sept.1913); in all some 223 pages.

Preliminary Check List of Zulu Names of Plants, appearing periodically in
'B. St.'[1] from 1938 onwards.

Since 1860 numerous works have been published dealing with Zulu grammar. In 1870 Bishop (then Canon) Callaway wrote an interesting contribution to the 'Natal Witness' entitled Some Remarks on the Zulu Language. This appraisement of the value of Zulu as a vehicle of thought was republished in pamphlet form in the same year.

Charles Roberts first issued The Zulu-Kafir Language simplified for Beginners[2] in 1874 from Mt. Coke Mission Press. This elementary study, with exercises and vocabularies, served a very useful purpose and went through a number of editions.[3] Much about this time he also published his Step-by-Step in Zulu[4]. A companion volume to his 'Zulu-Kafir Language' appeared in 1900, A Zulu Manual or Vade-Mecum[5]. This gave supplementary grammatical and syntactical information as well as certain specialised vocabularies.

In 1890 Ambrosius published at Mariannhill Trappist Monastery his Grammatik der Zulu-Kaffrischen Sprache (für den Schulgebrauch und Privatstudium)[6]. This is a fairly full exposition of the grammatical structure, but the handling and treatment are according to European preconceptions, for instance five 'cases' of nouns are treated. In 1895 Mariannhill issued (without author's name) an Elementar-grammatik der Zulu-Kaffrischen Sprache[7], with a large number of reading and translational exercises, as a complement to Ambrosius' Grammar. A very interesting publication was M. Dahle's Kortfattet Zulugrammatik[8] of 1893. This is the second Norwegian Zulu Grammar, the first being Schreuder's of 1850.[9] Dahle did not use Schreuder's strange orthography, but followed to a certain extent that in vogue at the time, using disjunctive word-division. His little work was designed for the use of Norwegian missionaries and colonists. It is not devoid of mistakes. In 1902 came a third Norwegian publication in O.S.Steenberg's Grundtraek of Zulu Sproget[10], published at Stavanger.

Quite a number of little books to aid the quick study of Zulu for practical purposes have been published in English. The first of these was by F. Mayr, Zulu Simplified, published during the last decade of the

---

1 Vol.XII, pp. 215-236, 321-342; XIII, pp. 49-64, 131-149, 307-326; XV, pp. 277-301, etc.
2 pp. vii + 145.
3 2nd ed. 1880; 3rd ed. (enlarged) 1895, of which a third impression appeared in 1902, a fourth in 1904 and a fifth in 1909.
4 I have not seen a copy of this.
5 pp. viii + 153.
6 pp. xii + 210, with folding tables.
7 pp. 128.
8 pp. ii + 91.
9 Cf. 'Bantu Pioneers', p.231.
10 I have not seen a copy of this.

century.[1] The grammatical part with exercises was followed by very useful English-Zulu conversations and idiomatic phrases. About 1935 the grammatical and exercise part alone (revised) was published, without author's name, by Shuter and Shooter, Maritzburg. In 1900 came <u>Zulu Self-taught with Key</u>[2] by Fred Eyles, and in 1907 the first edition of P. A. Stuart's <u>A Zulu Grammar for Beginners</u>[3] was published. In this grammatical rules were set out in a rough-and-ready, often inaccurate, manner, the new decisions of the 1907 Zulu Orthography Conference were embodied, and phrases and vocabularies added. The second edition, 1912, was entitled <u>Stuart's Zulu Course, Part I</u> (Part II has never come!). A third edition, bearing the same title as the first, and revised slightly, was published in 1932[4]. Soon after Stuart's second edition, came F. Suter's <u>Lessons in Zulu</u>, a simple little grammatical study which has been fairly popular and has seen a number of reprints.[5] A.T.Bryant published in 1909 a useful little volume, <u>Incwadi Yesingisi Nesizulu: Zulu without a Grammar, an English-Zulu Phrase-Book</u>. Brother Otto of Mariannhill had produced in 1907 his <u>Zulu Konstruktive Elemente</u>[6], a study based on interlinear translation into German.

Reference has already been made to W. Wanger's valuable lexicographical contributions in a specialist way. His greatest contribution to Zulu came, however, with the publication in 1917 of his large <u>Konversations-Grammatik der Zulu-Sprache</u>[7]. This is a mine of most valuable material, replete with idiomatic illustrations and a full study of the syntax of the language. German scholarship has been fully expended on the wealth of detail presented in this book. Wanger has used an almost complete conjunctive method of word-division,[8] but his grammatical approach is still insufficiently Bantu in character. In 1927 appeared Volume one of an ambitious scheme, Wanger's <u>Scientific Zulu Grammar</u>.[9] This book has been carried out with scholarly approach in many respects. Dealing with phonetics and the noun, it contains much new material and many valuable suggestions. The detailed treatment of Zulu prefixal formatives is

---

1 The second edition was in 1899, 5th 1904 and 6th 1910 (reprinted several times), pp.119 with vocabs. pp.ix appended.
2 pp.147.
3 pp.ix + 158.
4 and a fourth in 1940.
5 all undated, pp. vi + 135.
6 pp.84.
7 pp.15 + lxxi + 681.
8 In his 'Scientific Zulu Grammar', page 55, he discusses 'Conjunctivism, i.e. the method of joining into one word all those elements which in <u>native mentality and native pronunciation</u> form a unit having one principal accent,' and says, 'From a <u>scientific</u> point of view, there is no need to defend conjunctivism. And from a <u>practical</u> point of view, it seems useless to refute disjunctivism.' But it has been refuted since.
9 pp.xix + 346; no further volume has appeared, though three were planned.

especially meritorious. It is a valuable book of reference. It is seriously marred, however, by its arbitrary statement of 'phonetic laws', occupying pages 9 to 43, by which, for purposes of etymological gymnastics, any one sound is proved to be equal to practically any other. As an instance of this faulty treatment of sound-shifting, Wanger shows z to be equal, in turn, to c, gcw, d, nd, hl, dhl, nhl, j, nj, m, p, q, ng, s, t, ts, tsh, v, and y.[1] Building on such impossible premises as these, Wanger then introduced extensive comparisons with ancient Sumerian, further spoiling his grammar with the thesis of a Sumerian derivation for Zulu and indeed all Bantu. This thesis was carried forward ad nauseam in his 1935 publication, Comparative Lexical Study of Sumerian and Ntu ('Bantu'), in which he characterises Sumerian as the 'Sanscrit of the African Ntu Languages'. The whole thesis is built up on an unsound and unscientific phonetic basis, and will not stand detailed scrutiny.

Two little books might be mentioned here. In 1920 Alice Werner wrote a little book of Zulu Exercises[2]; and in 1921 M.F.W. published Elementary Zulu[3], a course of lessoss for beginners. Carl Faye included some interesting lexical material in his Zulu References for Interpreters and Students published in 1923; valuable textual material in the form of specimen speeches was also included. His brother, C.U.Faye, published in 'B.S.O.S.'[4] in 1925 an informative paper entitled The Influence of 'Hlonipa' on the Zulu Clicks. In 1925, R.C.A. Samuelson entered the grammatical field with his Zulu Grammar[5], which contributed nothing new to our knowledge of Zulu.

In 1927, urged by a need for a text book for University studies, C.M. Doke published the first edition of his Text Book of Zulu Grammar[6]. Conjunctive writing was used, and a modified phonetic orthography, designed to give a lead to the orthography discussions which were at that time beginning. A second edition was published in 1931 and a third in 1939, in which the accepted new orthography for Zulu is used. The main contribution in the book was, however, a new grammatical classification and treatment designed to get away from European and classical preconceptions, and use a mould more naturally suited to the structure of Bantu languages. The complete 'conjunctive' word was therefore taken as the basis for determining the parts of speech; such terms as 'preposition', 'case', 'comparison of adjectives', etc. were definitely discarded, and new terms including 'copulative', and ultimately 'ideophone' and 'deficient verb' found their place. The book has been widely adopted in training schools and educational work in Natal, and the methods advocated in it have found acceptance among workers in other language areas also. In 1932 Doke and Grant published a little supplementary volume of Graded Zulu Exercises[7] based on the text-

---

1 See pp. 42, 43.
2 pp. 51 including blank pages for class notes.
3 pp. 106.
4 Vol.III, Part IV, pp.757-782.
5 pp. 322.
6 pp. xii + 341.
7 pp. 56.

book. In 1933 G.C.S.Mdhladhla, a Supervisor of Native Schools, and A.H.S. Mbata, a Head Teacher in Natal, published a very creditable work, A Zulu Manual for Native Primary Schools.[1] This is a welcome sign of Native initiative, and testifies to the virility of the Zulu language. In 1943 a practical book for Afrikaans-speaking students of Zulu, Zoeloe-leerboek[2], was published by J.A.Engelbrecht. This introduced several features of value in a graded study of the language, and included appended vocabularies.

Three books have been produced in Zulu vernacular dealing with grammatical studies. The first was a little book of 34 pages by O.Stavem, published in Bishop Schreuder's orthography at 'Kristiania' in 1886 — Inṱela jolimi i loṱelwe abafana ba kwa Zulu, aba funda esikoleni. Latin terminology was used. The second was Igrama Lesizulu[3] by A.R. Kempe and H.K. Leisegang, published in 1922. This is a remarkable little book, but its use of Latin-English terminology is too unwieldy for practical usefulness. The following passage is typical: 'Ipasti futuri li patwa eindikativi kupela; l'enziwa ngokubeka ipasti li ka ba pambi kweverbi elikulu, lisemudi lerelativi efuturi.'[4] Anyone who is in a position to understand such a statement as that could understand far more easily a grammar written in English. The third, also called Igrama Lesizulu, written by H. Wiese in 1933, is a much smaller book[5], and uses the same type of terminology.

Zulu phonetics has drawn considerable attention. In 1923 C.M. Doke contributed to the 'B.S.O.S.'[6] A Dissertation on the Phonetics of the Zulu Language. This was followed by a much fuller monograph on the subject, The Phonetics of the Zulu Language[7], a doctor's thesis presented in 1924 and published in 1926. This was a work of descriptive phonetics based on considerable experimental work. A deep analysis of the tone-system, recorded by means of the numbers 1 to 9 above the syllables, was made. The system of the International Phonetic Association was adopted and somewhat modified for details. Questions of word-division, orthography and grammatical classification were touched upon. The book, though now out of print, has been widely used in advanced phonetic and Nguni studies in South Africa. Meanwhile, in 1924, C.Meinhof had published in the 'Z.E.S.'[8] an article Zur Lautlehre des Zulu in which he dealt with Zulu phonology historically in relation to the sounds postulated for Ur-Bantu. This article was subsequently, in 1932, incorporated in his Bantu-Phonology, translated by N.J. van Warmelo. In 1933 E.W. Selmer published at Oslo

---

1 pp.100.
2 pp.99.
3 pp. iv + 181.
4 page 97.
5 pp.32.
6 Vol.II, Part IV, pp.685–729.
7 pp.xii + 310.
8 Vol.XIV, pp.241–287.

his Experimentelle Beiträge zur Zulu Phonetik[1], a kymographic study of certain of the sounds.

The deliberations and recommendations of the Central Orthography Committee delegated by the Union Advisory Committee on Bantu Studies and Research resulted in the publication of two pamphlets, an interim one in 1929, Recommendations on Zulu Orthography[2], and the final findings in 1931, A Practical Orthography for Zulu[3]. These, with some slight modifications, have formed the official orthography of Zulu for educational and literary purposes. Orthography had long been a bone of contention among Zulu writers. L. Grout had written on the subject as early as 1852[4] and dissension had followed. An orthography conference had met in 1906 and another in 1907, which latter resulted in a lengthy publication, Report of Proceedings of Zulu Orthography Conference held at Durban, Natal, South Africa, May 29, 30, 31, 1907[5]. The main result of this was the adoption by a majority vote of disjunctive writing[6] for Zulu. On account of this decision three pages of rules, 18 paragraphs, were necessary to give guidance. The 1931 findings reversed this decision and introduced conjunctive writing, which needed no rules — only common sense!

It might be interesting to note that Zulu is the only Bantu language, as far as we know, that has attracted the attention of Russian writers. Professor I.L. Sneguireff[7] has written two articles on the language; one in the journal of the Marr Academy of Leningrad in Russian entitled (in French translation) Le nombre des préfixes nominaux dans la langue Zoulou[8] in 1933. The other, in the same year, appeared in the Bulletin of the Academy of Sciences of the U.S.S.R.[9]

The most important dialect of Zulu is Rhodesian Ndebele spoken in Matabeleland centring in Bulawayo, Southern Rhodesia. This dialect is used by somewhat under 200,000 speakers and is still used as an education and literary medium particularly by the London Missionary Society. In 1893 M.E. Weale published Matabele and Makalaka Vocabularies[10], a little

---

1   pp. 57.
2   pp. 7.
3   pp. 9.
4   Cf. 'Bantu Pioneers,' p. 229.
5   pp. 114. The report of the 1906 conference was printed by the Ebenezer Press, Dundee, Natal as a 15-page pamphlet.
6   J. Stuart had published for the 1906 conference Notes on the Conjunctive and Disjunctive Methods of writing Zulu, a 26-page pamphlet.
7   Sneguireff also translated into Russian Callaway's 'Nursery Tales of the Amazulu', and wrote articles on Communistic newspapers and terminology especially in Zulu, and on certain aspects of Bantu phonology.
8   In the section 'Le Langage et la Mentalité', pp. 29-36.
9   1933 volume, pp. 631-645.
10 pp. 32.

work arranged in three parallel columns, 'English, Tabele and Kalaka'. W.A. Elliott was the next exponent of the language, publishing in 189- his <u>Dictionary of the Tebele and Shuna Languages</u>[1]. The introductory part of this book contained some thirty pages of comparative grammatical material; then came an 'English-Tebele-Shuna' Vocabulary (pp.1-179), 'Tebele-English' Vocabulary (pp.180-257), 'Shuna-English Vocabulary' (pp.258-398); and 'Illustrative Sentences' (pp.399-441). A reprint published in 1897 omitted the last section, though leaving it referred to in the contents, and ended at page 398. Elliott's knowledge and treatment of the Ndebele part were superior to that of the Shona, which was very faulty. In 1911 Elliott wrote his <u>Notes for a Sindebele Dictionary and Grammar</u>.[2]

In 1912 appeared <u>A Grammar of the Sindebele Dialect of Zulu</u>[3] by J. O'Neil. This has proved a very useful and straightforward, albeit simple, exposition of the grammar with numerous examples and exercises. O'Neil had preceded this in 1909 with <u>A Phrase Book in English and Sindebele with a full Vocabulary</u>[4]; this has also been a very useful little book.

It is very questionable whether separate linguistic and literary work should be continued in a dialect so little different from Zulu.

Of <u>Transvaal Ndebele</u>, spoken in the Northern and Eastern Transvaal, the only publication dealing with the language is N.J. van Warmelo's <u>Transvaal Ndebele Texts</u> published in 1930. Pages 24-32 deal with the orthography, phonology and a short grammatical outline.

The <u>Ngoni</u> dialect, spoken in Nyasaland and parts of Southern Tanganyika, was first illustrated by Dr. W.A. Elmslie in his <u>Table of Concords, etc. of the Ngoni Language</u>, and his <u>Introductory Grammar of the Ngoni Language, as spoken in West Nyasaland</u>[5], both published in 1891. The Tanganyika dialect was treated by C. Spiss in his <u>Kingoni und Kisutu</u>, published in the 'M.S.O.S.' in 1904. The first thirty pages of this article comprise a grammatical outline of Ngoni; vocabularies German-Ngoni-Sutu follow this.

It remains to make mention of the pidgin tongue <u>Kitchen-Kafir</u>, which owes a large portion of its vocabulary to Zulu and Xhosa. O.O. Trapp contributed <u>Die Isikula-Sprache in Natal, Südafrika</u> to 'Ant.'[6] in 1908. B.G. Lloyd put out, through the Central News Agency, Johannesburg, his <u>Kitchen-Kafir Grammar and Vocabulary</u>, weird and amusing; for 'to nurse', for instance, we get 'Basop pikanin'. This booklet went through several editions.[7] The Prevention of Accidents Committee of the Rand Mutual Assurance Co., Ltd., published in 1920 a <u>Miners' Companion in Zulu</u>[8], in

---

1 pp.xxxix + 441.
2 I have not seen a copy of this.
3 pp.xii + 177.
4 pp.xi + 104; it went through a second edition at least.
5 pp.x, 51.
6 Vol.III, Part 3, pp.508-511.
7 The third, undated, has pp.48.
8 pp.40.

which a short exposition of Zulu for mine use is followed by phrases in English, Zulu and Kitchen-Kafir. A second edition entitled Miners' Companion in English, Afrikaans, Sesuto and Mine Kaffir[1] was published in 1938.

(b) Xhosa is spoken in the Eastern Cape Province. The earlier (pre-1860) linguistic work of Bennie, Boyce, Davis, Ayliff and Appleyard has already been noticed.[2] W.J. Davis, who edited Boyce's second edition in 1844 spanned over this period, and produced in 1872 his Grammar of the Kaffir Language[3], which was really a fourth edition of Boyce. Davis's grammar held the field for a considerable time; it was more concise than Appleyard's and favoured for practical purposes. In the same year, 1872, Davis published what might rightly be considered the earliest real dictionary of Xhosa, A Dictionary of the Kaffir Language: including the Xosa and Zulu Dialects. Part I Kafiir-English[4]. In this the words are dealt with etymologically, meanings are carefully discussed and numerous illustrative sentences are included. It is comparable in style to Döhne's Zulu Dictionary. Part II, An English and Kaffir Dictionary[5], came out in 1877. This was really a very large vocabulary with certain idiomatic illustrations; while principally dealing with Xhosa, it also included certain Zulu words. In 1903 this work was revised and enlarged by W. Hunter.[6]

In 1862 J.A. Bonatz wrote Anleitung zur Erlernung der Kaffer-Sprache[7], a study based on Appleyard's grammar. In 1874 Roberts wrote a Grammatical Note[8] on the language. In 1886 J. Torrend, well-known later for his 'Comparative Grammar', published his Outline of a Xosa-Kafir Grammar (with a few dialogues and a Kafir Tale)[9]. This little book, which already reflected signs of the author's spirit of deep enquiry, was in the press when J. McLaren published his An Introductory Kafir Grammar with Progressive Exercises[10] (1886). As he states in his introduction McLaren followed the system of Bleek in numbering the noun classes, keeping singulars and plurals separate; he also broke away from references to cases of nouns, and, in many ways, his work is an improvement on the grammars then in use. This was published at Lovedale. A second edition, entitled A Grammar of the Kaffir Language, entirely revised and rewritten, was published by Longmans in 1906, and a further slightly revised form[11] of

---

1 pp.114.
2 Cf. 'Bantu Pioneers', pp.216-221, 223-226.
3 Cf. 'Bantu Pioneers', p.220; this edition had pp.viii + 183.
4 pp.viii + 260 (double col.).
5 pp.xiv + 232 (wrongly printed 332).
6 pp.v + 499. A further edition was published as recently as 1922.
7 pp.xii + 292.
8 I have not seen this, but take it to be Charles Roberts who published the first edition of his Zulu Grammar in the same year.
9 pp.95.
10 pp.viii + 112.
11 pp.xiv + 240.

this appeared in 1917. McLaren's was the standard Xhosa grammar used for educational purposes for many years. McLaren died in 1934 while still at work revising his grammar. The new edition, entitled A Xhosa Grammar,[1] was edited by G.H. Welsh and published in 1936. This was in the new Xhosa orthography; it contained a fuller phonological treatment, a re-numbering of the noun-classes to bring them into line with what had been adopted in Zulu, and a more up-to-date nomenclature and classification, including a valuable treatment of deficient verbs; ideophones, though referred to on page 135, are, however, very inadequately treated. This is still the standard reference book for Xhosa grammar.

A little vocabulary and phrase-book, prepared by A.J. Newton was printed at 'S. Peter's-on-Indwe' in 1885[2], Lessons in Words and Phrases in English and Kafir[3]. This is a rare little item. A book which, for many years, was popular for picking up a smattering of Xhosa was A First Kafir Course by C.J. Crawshaw. The first edition[4] appeared in 1888, the second in 1894, the third in 1897, a fourth in 1901. It was a practical course, with exercises — good as far as it goes. In 1887 E. Nagel published his little Praktisches Hülfsbuch der Kaffern-Sprache of some 43 pages.

James Stewart of Lovedale made his contribution to Xhosa studies. In 1894 he published Practical Exercises in Kaffir, with the Essential Portions of the Kaffir Verb.[5] Shortly afterwards[6] he published in compact form his Outlines of Kaffir Grammar[7]. These two publications were united in 1901 in Stewart's well-known Outlines of Kaffir Grammar with Practical Exercises[8], which was intended to serve Native students in institutions; it was unfortunately rather spoiled in later editions by faulty editing. In 1899 Stewart published his Kaffir Phrase Book and Vocabulary[9], a book which for long had a very wide vogue, and went through many editions.[10]

The latest grammatical study, and one of the most interesting, is W.G. Bennie's A Grammar for the Xhosa-Speaking[11], published in 1939. It is prepared with up-to-date methods and presented in a pleasing conversational style. In this valuable contribution we get a discussion of

1 pp.xvi + 248.
2 Or 1884; a 5th edition revised came as early as 1894.
3 pp.40.
4 pp.viii + 133.
5 pp.46 + 23 pages of verb (unnumbered).
6 Date not known, my copy is without title-page.
7 pp.104.
8 pp.vii+ 223.
9 pp.iv + 134.
10 For instance: 3rd ed. 1901, 4th ed. (without vocab.) 1903, 6th ed. (ditto) 1906, 8th ed. (ditto, pp.64) 1916, 8th ed. (full) 1916, 11th ed. (without vocab.) 1928.
11 pp.5 + 169.

grammatical and syntactical forms of value to those who already speak Xhosa. The presentation is therefore different from that in other grammars, vocabulary examples are not so numerous and certain knowledge is taken for granted.

Modern Xhosa lexicography is principally indebted to A. Kropf, who published his Kaffir-English Dictionary[1] in 1899. This is a masterly study. Kropf shewed sound lexicographical method when he remarked[2], 'The words have been arranged in alphabetical order of the stem or root'; and though he grouped verb derivatives before noun derivatives from a common stem despite alphabetical order, his method of entry made reference fairly easy. He, however, carried derivative entries too far, including many forms the meanings of which can be deduced by the regular rules. Among the same remarks he raised the difficult question of the place of dividing prefix from stem, the point of division often being different from that employed in the ordinary reading and writing of Xhosa. Much valuable idiomatic material is included as illustration in this dictionary. A second edition[3], revised, added to and greatly improved by R.Godfrey, was published in 1915. This contained a valuable introduction dealing with derivative forms. A third edition of this great work is awaiting completion and publication. J. McLaren's contribution to Xhosa studies was most effective also in dictionary work. In 1915 he put out A Concise Kaffir-English Dictionary[4], a very useful book of reference, which was revised and edited as a second edition by W.G.Bennie in the new orthography in 1936 under the title of A Concise Xhosa-English Dictionary[5]. This is a sound, reliable book of ready reference. In 1923 McLaren published A Concise English-Kafir Dictionary[6], a full and trustworthy explanation of English words, one of the best English-Bantu dictionaries yet published, and fully comparable to Madan's Swahili work. McLaren's trilogy, the grammar and the two dictionaries, constitutes a most valuable Xhosa contribution. In regard to specialised dictionaries mention should here be made of Neil Macvicar's An English-Kafir Nurses' Dictionary, a small but useful work dealing with the equivalents to medical terms. In 1917 T.R.L.Kingon contributed Some Place-names of Tsolo to the 'S.A. Journal of Science'[7]. A far more important and valuable work is R. Godfrey's Bird-lore of the Eastern Cape Province, published as a 'Bantu Studies Monograph' (No. 2) in 1941. This is a cyclopaedic dictionary of bird names principally in Xhosa. Originally the embryo of this work appeared periodically in the 'Blythswood Review'.

---

1 Lovedale, pp.vii + 486 (large, double col.).
2 on page v.
3 pp.xxxii + 525 (large, double col.).
4 pp.xv +194 (double col.).
5 pp.xix +197 (double col.).
6 pp.viii +320 (double col.).
7 pp.17.

W. Bourquin made some small scientific contributions to our knowledge of Xhosa grammar in his papers, <u>Adverb und adverbiale Umschreibung im Kafir</u>, a most exhaustive study contributed to the 'Z.f.K.S.'[1] between 1912 and 1914, and <u>The Prefix of the Locative in Kafir</u>, written for 'B.St.'[2] in 1922, in which an attempt is made to discover the origin of the locative prefix. In 1903 I.Bud-M'Belle published his <u>Kafir Scholar's Companion</u>[3]. This is rather a hotch-potch of information, some of it certainly useful, but much, particularly his large section of 'Syllabic words', of little practical value. He has an interesting opening section dealing with 'Kafir Literature', as well as a bibliography of publications dealing with the Native races. In 1905 C.Meinhof published his authoritative <u>Hottentottische Laute und Lehnworte im Kafir</u>, which had appeared in Volumes LVIII and LIX of the 'Z.D.M.G.'[4].

In the field of phonetics the only special contribution to be noticed is D.M. Beach's <u>The Science of Tonetics and its Application to Bantu Languages</u> in 'B.St.'[5] in 1924. This is an extremely valuable introduction to the study of Tone, with a special application to an analysis of Xhosa. Doke gave a short analysis of Xhosa phonetics in Appendix No.VII[6] to his 'Phonetics of the Zulu Language'. Good phonetic introductions were given by Welsh in his editing of McLaren's grammar, and by Bennie in his editing of McLaren's dictionary and in his own 'Grammar for the Xhosa-Speaking'.

The new Xhosa orthography is represented in literature by a pamphlet issued by the Union Government Advisory Committee on Bantu Studies and Research, <u>A Practical Orthography for Xhosa</u>[7], 1931. This was prepared by W.G. Bennie, as was also <u>Notes on the New Xhosa Orthography</u>[8] issued from Lovedale in connection with their publications, 'The Stewart Readers', etc., in the new orthography. This latter is a lucid explanation of the position.

Upon the literature as a whole in Xhosa, reference may be made to R. Godfrey's article <u>Rev. John Bennie, the Father of Kafir Literature</u>, which was published in 'B.St.'[9] in 1934; and to the 'Preliminary Investigation' in 'B.St.'[10] in 1933. An article by R.Godfrey in the 'Blythswood Review' of June 1931 is also very informative.

---

1 Vol.3, pp.230-243, 279-326; Vol.4, pp.68-74, 118-155, 231-248 (in all some 125 pages).
2 Vol.I, No.2, pp.2,3.
3 pp.xxiii, 181.
4 Vol.LVIII, pp.727-769, and Vol.LIX, pp.36-89.
5 Vol.II, pp.75-106.
6 <u>The Phonetic Peculiarities of Xosa (ukuteta)</u>, pp.305-307.
7 pp.8.
8 pp.22.
9 Vol.8, pp.123-134.
10 See particularly pp.40-46 of Vol.VII.

In regard to Xhosa dialects there are two little studies on Mpondo: F. Bachmann's Wörterbuch Deutsch-Pondo[1], published in the 'Z.A.S.' 1888, and Beste's Zusätze und Berichtigungen zum Pondo-Wörterbuch[2] in the same journal, 1889-90, adding to Bachmann's work. In 1927 W. Bourquin contributed to the 'Festschrift Meinhof'[3] a phonological study on the Meinhof pattern entitled Die Sprache der Phuthi. The Phuthi speak a dialectal form of Xhosa.

(c) Swazi, spoken in Swaziland, apart from H.H. Johnston's vocabularies, has not yet had its grammar seriously treated in any published work. J.A. Engelbrecht added some grammatical notes to his Swazi Texts with Notes, published in 1930 in the 'Annals of the University of Stellenbosch';[4] and D. Ziervogel gave a Kort Oorsig van die Klanke en die Vormleer van Swazi in the first eight pages of his 'Swazi-Gebruike vanaf Geboorte tot Huwelik', published in 1944. We have no records of the allied Old Mfengu or of Baca, apart from MS. works on the latter by D.P. Hallowes and A.C. Jordan.

(2) Sotho Group. This group is divided into four cluster sections, of which Southern Sotho, the most important from the point of view of literature, is probably almost as recent in formation as Kololo, the least important. Each of these four are today being used as distinct literary media, though, from that point of view, Kololo might practically be disregarded.

(a) Northern Sotho, confined to the Transvaal, central, northern and eastern districts. The literary form is based almost entirely upon the biggest dialect, Pedi. The most important worker in this type of Sotho was K. Endemann, who published his 'classical and standard' work on the grammar of the language in 1876, under the title of Versuch einer Grammatik des Sotho[5]. He used an orthography of his own based on the Lepsius' system. The grammatical analysis and terminology are somewhat antiquated, but they are very full and accurate. The work treats mainly of Pedi but includes reference to Tswana and Southern Sotho. Endemann's great Wörterbuch der Sotho-Sprache appeared in 1911. This great work of 727 pages (double col.) is not so generally acclaimed as the grammar. Here again the author uses a phonetic spelling of his own with the basic intonation of most of the words given, though this is not always reliable. Besides Northern Sotho, much is drawn from Tswana and Southern Sotho, dialectal variants being generally indicated. Jacottet, the Southern Sotho scholar, paid high tribute to the 'Versuch', but wrote a rather scathing

---

1 Jahrg. 3, pp. 40-76.
2 Jahrg. 3, pp. 235-240.
3 pp. 279-287.
4 Vol. VIII, Sectn. B, No. 2, pp. 1-21.
5 pp. 201. Previously, in 1872, Endemann had given a grammatical sketch of the language of 22 pages in his Mitteilungen über die Sotho-Neger in the 'Z.f.E.'.

criticsm[1] of Endemann's method of handling the dictionary work, in which he says he has embodied material from Mabille's and Brown's dictionaries without any acknowledgement. This work, however, is of special importance, because it was the first considerable dictionary to make an attempt at consistent marking of the tones. The dictionary, however, lacked idiomatic illustrations. In 1899 C. Meinhof included a chapter on 'Pedi' phonology in his 'Lautlehre der Bantusprachen'. Here the language is brought into comparison with his postulation for Ur-Bantu.

In 1920 G. Beyer wrote a little Handbook of the Pedi-Transvaal-Suto Language[2] using the spelling of the 1910 agreement. This was a little practical grammar with exercises, phrases, dialogues and vocabularies. About 1924 G.H. Franz and T.P. Mathabathe published An Outline of English-Transvaal-Sesotho Grammar and Composition[3], written partly in English and partly in Sotho, and intended for Native school use; it contains useful information on idiom and syntax. About the same time, also undated, the same authors published A Vocabulary of the more common words in the Transvaal-Sesotho Language[4]. G.H. Franz, about 1931, produced Thellenyane[5], a useful little beginner's book for Afrikaans speakers learning Northern Sotho, and about the same time Motsoša-Lenyôra, Seripa saI, saII[6] (The Slaker of Thirst, Part I, II). These little books written in Sotho (new orthography) present a series of exercises upon the grammar and composition of Northern Sotho for Native School children. They are based upon the direct method of mother-tongue teaching and are well suited to their purpose. P.E. Schwellnus, also about 1931, published his Thlalosa-Polêlô: Grammar ya Sesotho se se bolêlwaxo dileteng tša Transvaal (The Explainer of Language)[7]. This vernacular grammar of Northern Sotho links up with the two exercise books of Franz. It attempts to supply Sotho equivalents for the various technical terms employed; is short and elementary, but accurate and systematic. With 1939 came an important publication, T.M.H. Endemann's Handleiding by die aanleer van Transvaal-Sotho (Sepedi)[8]. This marks the scientific interest being taken in Bantu languages, especially in the Sotho group, by young Afrikaans graduates. Endemann's is a good piece of work, containing a sound phonetic analysis of the language. Accompanying this was his Sotho-Woordelys,[9] a Northern Sotho-Afrikaans Vocabulary of useful size. A bigger vocabulary of considerable importance was published by T.J. Kriel in 1932: Sotho-Afrikaanse Woordeboek.[10] H.J. van Zyl made a very useful practical contribution to Northern Sotho studies

---

1 Cf. Intro. to his Grammar of the Sesuto Language, pp.xvii, xviii.
2 pp.99.
3 pp.112.
4 pp.69.
5 pp.77.
6 Pt.I, pp.31, Pt.II, pp.35.
7 pp.71.
8 pp.157.
9 pp.56 (double col.)
10 pp.219.

in 1941 with his Thika Polēlō[1] (Wholesale attack on speech), a vernacular study and exercise book designed for use in Teachers' Training Colleges. Other similar studies are Kxaša-Peu I[2], prepared in 1940 by the Teachers of Pax College, and M.J.S. Madiba's Thutō ya Polēlō[3] of 1941.

Regarding more general linguistic subjects mention might be made of W.Eiselen's Zur Erforschung des Lovelu-dialektes, a comparative phonetic analysis followed by texts, which appeared in 1928 in the 'Z.E.S.'[4] In 1932 A.N. Tucker contributed to the 'M.S.O.S.'[5] an article entitled Some Little Known Dialects of SePedi. Tucker further wrote a memorandum for the International Institute of African Languages and Cultures (c.1929) on Suggestions for the Spelling of Transvaal Sesuto.[6] This antedated the orthography conferences on the subject, but had little influence upon the ultimate decisions which were embodied in a pamphlet authorised by the Union Advisory Committee on African Studies and Research in South Africa, and drawn up by G.P. Lestrade — The Practical Orthography of Transvaal Sotho, reprinted from 'B.St.'[7] in 1930. Tucker had done far more valuable work in his 'Comparative Phonetics' (1929), of which more presently. T.M.H. Endemann's Palatalisering en Labialisering in Sepedi[8] is a comparative study of considerable importance.

(b) Southern Sotho, or 'Sesotho sa haMoshoeshoe', spoken in Basutoland and the eastern parts of the Orange Free State, was to a certain extent dealt with by E. Casalis in his Etudes sur la Langue Séchuana of 1841[9]. Jacottet[10] refers to 'a long grammatical note on Sesuto' written by Ch. Schrumpf in the 'Z.D.M.G.' in 1862.

The first definite Southern Sotho grammatical work, however, was that of A. Mabille, who published in 1878 his Helps for to learn the Sesuto Language[11], of which Jacottet[12] wrote: 'It is a little book which does not pretend in the least to give a scientific exposition of the language... But it is complete as far as it goes and quite reliable. It is even today[13] a mine of materials useful for a better treatment of Sesuto. Although now superseded and out of print for more than forty years, it is a most useful book and subsequent authors like Kruger and

---

1 pp.149.
2 pp.194.
3 pp.93.
4 Vol.XIX, pp.98–116.
5 Vol.XXXV, pp.133–142.
6 pp.23.
7 Vol.IV, pp.1–9.
8 Cyclostyled foolscap, pp.65.
9 Referred to in 'Bantu Pioneers', p.221.
10 On p.xiv of the introduction to his 'Grammar of the Sesuto Language'.
11 Printed at Morija, pp.223, 9.5 x 13 cms.
12 On pp.xiv, xv of the introduction to his 'Grammar of the Sesuto Language'.
13 Penned some time before 1920.

myself, are deeply indebted to it.' In the same year, 1878, F.H. Kruger brought out his Steps to Learn the Sesuto Language[1], which consisted of a very sound elementary grammar, graduated exercises and a short vocabulary. This work was an advance on Mabille's (of which Kruger but claimed his work to be a revision) and even on Endemann's 'Versuch', which Kruger consulted, in that the author endeavoured to give a thorough exposition of Sotho syntax. Jacottet entertained a very high opinion of Kruger's linguistic ability. Of him he wrote[2]: 'Mr. Kruger had passed barely 18 months in Basutoland when he composed his grammar. This explains some unavoidable errors and a sometimes too dogmatic tone. It is much to be regretted that Mr. Kruger's health obliged him to leave Basutoland after only a short stay. Had he remained we should have had in him the best possible Sesuto linguist. The present writer cannot express sufficiently his indebtedness to his gifted predecessor.'

In 1893 E. Jacottet published, as an introduction to the second edition of Mabille's 'Vocabulary', An Elementary Sketch of Sesuto Grammar, covering much the same ground as Kruger's work, without touching on the syntax. Jacottet, who did more than anyone else to encourage and foster the growth of a Native Sotho literature, became also its foremost grammarian. In 1906 he produced the first edition of his Practical Method to learn Sesuto[3], a book which has been, and is still being, used more than any other by students of the language. The 'Practical Method' went through a large number of editions until, in 1936, it was enlarged somewhat by additional material by H.E. Jankie. In 1908 Jacottet published his vernacular grammar for school use — Grammar e nyenyane ea Sesotho.[4] His death in 1920 deprived Basutoland of one of their greatest champions of literature. In 1927 C.M. Doke edited a manuscript left by Jacottet and this was published as a special number of 'B.St.' entitled A Grammar of the Sesuto Language[5]. Acknowledgement is made to considerable help from Z.D. Mangoaela in its composition, and this grammar, despite certain faults and omissions, has since been considered as the standard grammar of Southern Sotho. Jacottet used a system of diacritic marks on the vowels in this work which carefully distinguished them, what the present Sotho orthography represents by e and o, being differentiated into e, ĕ, è, ê and o, ō, ò, ŏ respectively: too cumbersome for practical purposes, but very valuable in a scientific work of reference. What is probably attributable to E. Casalis is a little book of Sesuto and English Exercises of about 50 pages[6].

---

1 A 2nd edition in 1883, 3rd ed. in 1904, and a 4th in 1905 (pp.viii+127).
2 On p. xv of the Introduction to his 'Grammar of the Sesuto Language'.
3 The 1914 edition was pp.viii + 232.
4 pp.vi + 70; in 1911 a book of Answers to the exercises in this was published, pp.54.
5 pp.xxvi + 209.
6 I do not know the date of publication; but the 7th ed. was 1901, the 11th 1930 and the 12th 1938.

One of the most recent Southern Sotho grammars is one in Afrikaans by C.F. de Jager, Handleiding by die Studie van Sesoeto op ons Skole[1], published in 1936. This is a good, sound piece of work and blazes a new trail in Afrikaans terminology for Bantu grammar; it is the first Bantu grammar to be written in Afrikaans medium. This was followed in 1941 by B.I.C. van Eeden's Inleiding tot die Studie van Suid-Sotho[2], which embodied much more up-to-date treatment of Sotho than any Sotho grammar had hitherto done. In it a chapter was devoted to the 'ideofoon' and a very full treatment of verbal derivatives given. In 1943 Van Eeden supplemented this with his Praktiese Suid-Sotho-Lesse.[3]

In Southern Sotho lexicography A. Mabille was the pioneer. In 1876 appeared his Sesuto-English Dictionary[4], really an extensive vocabulary. The second edition, of 1893, came out preceded by Jacottet's grammatical sketch and followed by an 'English-Sesuto Vocabulary', making a volume of 487 pages.[5] The Sotho-English part went through a number of editions[6], being continually expanded. The later editions were edited by H.Dieterlen, to whom the work owed much, and to whose wife we are indebted for a valuable addition of botanical terms. The English-Sesuto Vocabulary section also went through a number of editions.[7] The later editions were edited by A. Casalis and present a sound, reliable vocabulary. In 1891 Morija Mission published Mantsue a go Buisana ka se-Sotho le se-English, a 'dictionary of conversation'. This later became known as Puisana, the oft-reprinted and much-used phrase book — Sesotho-English.

Among other linguistic works on Southern Sotho deserving of notice are the following: In 1929 N.J. van Warmelo contributed to 'B.St.' an article on European and other Influences in Sotho[8]. At about the same time A.N. Tucker put out his Comparative Phonetics of the Suto-Chuana Group of Bantu Languages[9], a descriptive work of considerable value, giving detailed attention to questions of tonetics and special phonetic phenomena such as labialization. It treats of the three main Sotho types, using as basis the orthography of the International Phonetic Association. In 1938 G.P. Lestrade contributed to 'B.St.'[10] a valuable paper on Locative-class Nouns and Formatives in Sotho, also surveying the phenomena according to the

---

1 pp.313.
2 pp.283.
3 Practical Lessons, roneod pp.70.
4 pp.158. The Bibliography of the New York Public Library records under this date a Sesuto-English Vocabulary by F.H. Kruger, also of 158 pages.
5 of which 415 were of vocabularies in double column.
6 3rd ed. 1904; 4th ed. 1911; 5th ed. 1924, pp.viii + 535 (double col.); 6th ed. 1937.
7 2nd ed. 1905; 3rd ed. 1908; 4th ed. 1911 & 1915; 5th ed.1925 (pp.203).
8 Vol.III, pp.405-421.
9 Undated; pp.139.
10 Vol.XII, pp.35-62.

three main Sotho types.

(c) <u>Tswana</u>, with a large number of dialects, spoken in Bechuanaland Protectorate, British Bechuanaland, the Western Transvaal and the Western part of the Orange Free State.

After the early work of Archbell and Casalis, C. Schrumpf contributed a fairly long grammatical sketch on the language, referred to as 'Sesuto' in the 'Z.D.M.G.' in 1862; Jacottet does not speak highly of this. In 1864 J. Frédoux published in Cape Town <u>A Sketch of the Sechuana Grammar</u>, a little 12-page booklet, presenting the elements very concisely. Crisp gave considerable praise to this little work.

In 1876 John Brown of the London Missionary Society published a 'dictionary'[1] in two parts <u>Lokwalo loa Mahūkū a Secwana le Seeñeles</u> (Tswana-English) and <u>Secwana Vocabulary</u> (English-Tswana). A second edition of this entitled <u>Secwana Dictionary</u>[2] appeared in 1895 in which the 'English-Tswana' part came first. This was preceded by some 15 pages of 'Hints to learners of Secwana'. Reprints of this second edition came out in 1914 and 1921. But in 1923 J. Tom Brown re-edited, enlarged and greatly improved the work under the title <u>Secwana Dictionary, Secwana-English and English-Secwana</u>. Brown's basis was Tlhaping, and the latest edition in the orthography of 1910 is the standard dictionary of the language. It could be improved in explanation and illustrative sentences, but is fairly full and accurate.

W. Crisp did good grammatical work, mainly in the Tlaro dialect and Southern Rolong, when he produced in 1880 his <u>Notes towards a Secoana Grammar</u>,[3] printed at Bloemfontein. This is considered to be the best Tswana Grammar to date, both in analysis and phonetic transcription. A second edition appeared in 1886, third in 1900, fourth in 1905 and fifth in 1924. In 1905 A.J. Wookey produced his <u>Secwana Grammar with Exercises</u>.[4] Using the Tlhaping dialect as basis, Wookey produced a valuable sourcebook, containing a mass of material, which however was badly arranged. A second edition revised and enlarged, but not materially improved, by J.T. Brown, was issued in 1921. Much earlier on Wookey had produced his useful <u>Secwana and English Phrases</u>, 'with a short introduction to grammar (22 pages) and a vocabulary'. The second edition of this was issued in 1902 and a third in 1904. Two recent publications of the University of Cape Town, by I. Schapera and D.F. v.d. Merwe in collaboration, have added to our knowledge of some of the less-studied dialects. These are: <u>Notes on the Noun Classes of Some Bantu Languages of Ngamiland</u>[5], and <u>A Comparative Study of Kgalagadi, Kwena and other Sotho Dialects</u>.[6]

---

1 pp.viii + 279 + iv.
2 pp.466.
3 pp.100.
4 pp.232.
5 1942, pp.103 (roneod).
6 1943, pp.119 (roneod).

In regard to Phonetics and Orthography much information on Tswana is to be had in Tucker's Comparative Phonetics of the Suto-Chuana Group of Bantu Languages. Daniel Jones and S.T. Plaatje had issued in 1916 A Sechuana Reader[1] in International Phonetic Orthography preceded by a most valuable phonetic analysis. This was a pioneer effort. Daniel Jones further contributed Words distinguished by Tone in Sechuana to the 'Festschrift Meinhof'[2] in 1927, and The Tones of Sechuana Nouns[3] as Memorandum VI of the International Institute of African Languages and Cultures, 1929, which included division into intonation-classes, positional intonation-change, etc.

The present recognised Tswana Orthography was fixed at the Johannesburg Conference in 1937, the findings of which were embodied in A Practical Orthography for Tswana[4], compiled by G.P. Lestrade. This superseded a previous interim pamphlet, issued in 1930, entitled The Practical Orthography of Tswana[5].

(d) Kololo. This S.Sotho dialect with infiltration of Tswana, which became the language of Barotseland, was first illustrated by S. Colyer's Sikololo, Notes on the Grammar with a Vocabulary[6], published in 1914. This book contained a fair percentage of importations from the Lozi dialect, and the grammatical part was based on a manuscript by A. Jalla. In 1915 Stirke and Thomas produced a little Sikololo Phrase Book, and the next year a Comparative Vocabulary. But it is to Adolphe Jalla that we owe our knowledge of the language. In 1917 he published a useful little trilogy Sikololo-English Dictionary[7], English-Sikololo Dictionary[8], and Elementary Grammar of the Sikololo Language[9]. The grammar was modelled on Kruger's 'Steps' in Southern Sotho. In 1942 M. Gluckman contributed a short paper to 'African Studies'[10] entitled Prefix Concordance in Lozi, Lingua Franca of Barotseland.

(3) Venda, spoken in the Northern Transvaal up to and across the Limpopo River into Southern Rhodesia, has practically no distinctive dialectal forms, and is spoken by somewhat over 150,000 people.

In 1901 Meinhof published in the 'Z.D.M.G.'[11] a phonological study entitled Das Tsi-venda in which the sound-shiftings from his hypothetical Ur-Bantu are fully studied. In this there is very little tabulated grammatical material, but a short vocabulary in phonetic script. In 1904 in

1 pp.xl + 45.
2 pp.88—98.
3 pp.26.
4 'B.St.' Vol.XI, pp.137—148.
5 pp.11.
6 pp.53.
7 pp.205.
8 pp.159.
9 pp.102.
10 Vol.I, pp.105—114.
11 pp.607—682.

Volume VII of the 'M.S.O.S.'[1] appeared Die Verba des Tšivendá, by T. and P. Schwellnus; this is a small vocabulary in phonetic script with intonation marked. This had been preceded by the same author's Wörterverzeichnis der Venda-Sprache, which appeared in 1919 as a special number of Vol. XXXVI of the Jahrb. Hamb.Wiss.Anst.[2].

P. Schwellnus, known for his Bible translation and other literary work in Venda, published a little grammar[3] in the vernacular, entitled Luvenḓa Grammar or Phenḓa-luambo ya u ṭalukanya Tshivenḓa, in which he introduced an amount of grammatical terminology in Venda, English equivalents and explanations being freely added. This was followed in 1941 by T.M.H. Endemann and E.F.N. Mudau's Phenḓa-Luambo ya Zwikolo zwa Venda[4], based on the work of Schwellnus, but extended and giving exercises. In this the Venda terminology was used without English explanations. In 1936 L.T. Marole and F.J. de Gama had published quite a useful English-Tshivenda Vocabulary[5], in which an orthography devoid of diacritics was employed.

The most important dictionary of the language, however, was N.J. van Warmelo's Tshivenḓa-English Dictionary[6] which was published in 1937. This is a fairly full dictionary, with tone-markings on all the entries, preceded by a short grammatical outline.

Certain manuscript work has been used in missions and training centres for studying the language. I have before me Tshivenda Grammar Notes of 31 quarto typed pages, a simple exposition, author unknown. Then Ch. Endemann produced two manuscripts Versuch einer Venda-Grammatik, and an Afrikaans version Venda-Grammatika, containing some 71 pages of morphology and 16 of syntax[7]. F. Krüger also produced manuscripts which have been duplicated and used as text-books, viz. Penḓa-luambo ya Tshivenḓa and Tsumbanḓila.

There is an obvious need for a good grammatical exposition of Venda.

(4) **Tsonga Group (Shangana-Tonga)**:[8] Spoken in Portuguese East Africa from the Zululand border to the Sabi River and in the North-eastern sector

---

1 pp.12-31
2 pp.51-78.
3 pp.59, n.d.
4 pp.72.
5 pp.94.
6 Vol.VI of the 'Ethnological Publications' of the Union Dept. of Native Affairs, pp.345 (double col.).
7 For information on these see Lestrade's notes on p.88 of 'B.St.', Vol. VII, No.1.
8 For details of the literature of this Group, reference should be made to A.A. Jaques A Survey of Shangana-Tsonga, Ronga and Tswa Literature 'B.St.', Vol.XIV, pp.259-270.

of the Transvaal. Of the three main clusters in this group, Ronga, the language of Lourenço Marques, was the earliest dealt with.

A.A.P. Cabral included in his Vocabulário lists for 'Shironga' and 'Shitsua', as well as for 'Guitonga' and 'Shishope' (of Inhambane).

(a) Ronga: Bleek had included this language under the name 'Lourenço Marques' in his 1856 'Languages of Mosambique'. In 1893 Smith-Delacour (H.B.M. Consul at Lourenço Marques) published a little Shironga Vocabulary[1], said by H.H. Johnston to have been 'derived from the works of a native missionary'. Johnston criticises the work as 'misleading and incorrect'. The author uses a most weird method of indicating the pronunciation. In 1895 R. Paiva published a little 75-page handbook, entitled Noções de grammatica Landina[2] e breve guia de conversação em portuguez, inglez e landim. In the next year A.S. Pinheiro included Subsidios para a grammatica landina (Xijonga) de Lourenço Marques, as a fragment of 'Portugal em Africa'[3]. The standard grammatical work on the language, however, is that of H.A. Junod, Grammaire Ronga[4], which appeared in 1896. This is a straightforward exposition followed by a 'Manuel de Conversation' and a 'Vocabulaire ronga-portugais-français-anglais'. Junod was careful to use illustrative sentences freely and added some folklore textual material. In 1901 Paiva published in the Bulletin of the Soc. de Geographia de Lisboa[5] his Diccionario da lingua landina, português, inglês, landim...; and in 1903 Junod produced Bukhaneli bya Šironga[6], a grammar of Ronga in the vernacular for use in schools, where it has proved of value despite its close following of European structural methods. In 1906 E. Torre do Valle produced fairly comprehensive vocabularies entitled Diccionarios Shironga-Portuguez e Portuguez-Shironga[7], to which he prefaced a few pages of grammatical notes based on Junod's 'Grammaire'. In 1907 came P. Loze's little 24-page Vocabulario Portuguez-Shironga for Mission school use. In 1917 Father A.L. Farinha published his Elementos de Gramática Landina[8]. Besides a simple description of the grammatical elements, the author included some folk-tales in the vernacular, sentences in conversation and vocabularies (60 pages). The missionary P. Berthoud produced in 1920 his little Eléments de Grammaire Ronga[9], a simple outline. H.L. Bishop contributed a valuable paper on The Descriptive Com-

---

1 pp.31, preceded by a map of the district.
2 Using the term current for the language of that area.
3 pp.477-534.
4 pp.218 + 90.
5 Ser.18, Nos.2 and 3, pp.47-123.
6 pp.59.
7 pp.322.
8 pp.196.
9 pp.56.

plement in the Sironga Language to the 'South African Journal of Science'[1] in 1922. This is probably the first attempt to classify the ideophones in any Bantu language. He also wrote, On the Use of the Proclitic 'a' in Sironga, a short paper in 'B.St.'[2] in 1925. Among unpublished works is a Ronga-English Dictionary prepared by P. Loze and H.L. Bishop.

(b) Tonga: For this language, commonly called Shangaan', with its main dialect Gwamba, the earliest publication was P. Berthoud's little Leçons de Šigwamba of 1883, and his Grammatical Note on the Gwamba Language in South Africa, published in the Journal of the Royal Asiatic Society[3] in 1884; but our main authority is again H.A. Junod, the renowned author of 'The Life of a South African Tribe'. In 1903 he wrote a vernacular grammar entitled Vuvulavuri bya Šithonga, a translated parallel to his Ronga version, 'Bukhaneli', of the same year. A second edition[4] of this appeared in 1929. He followed this work in 1907 by his Elementary Grammar of the Thonga-Shangaan Language[5], a good exposition, only marred perhaps by a tendency to superficial treatment, exemplified by his dropping of the initial vowel of the noun-prefixes because of its irregularity and difficulty[6]. A second edition of this appeared in 1932. Meanwhile however the first had been issued bound as an introduction to Ch. W. Chatelain's Pocket Dictionary[7] (Thonga-English; English-Thonga), which was published in 1909. This short vocabulary has served a very useful purpose and saw a second edition in 1923 and a third in 1933. Part I of a lesson series, Step by Step in Thonga[8] prepared by C.A. Chawner appeared in roneo form in 1938.

In 1914 Paul Passy, the founder of the International Phonetic Association, gave a careful analysis and description of the sounds of this language in his La Langue Thonga, which appeared in 'Miscellanea Phonetica'. After P. Berthoud's death his little unfinished Shangaan Grammar[9] was published in 1920 in out-of-date orthography, which has detracted from an otherwise useful piece of work.

In 1927 W.M. Eiselen wrote an article on Nasalverbindungen im Thonga for the 'Festschrift Meinhof'[10], and N.J. van Warmelo gave a phonological analysis of Gwamba in his 'Die Gliederung der süd-afrikanischen Bantusprachen'[11] in 1927, following this with an article Zur Gwamba-Lautlehre in the 'Z.E.S.'[12] in 1930. These three studies present the subject ac-

---

1 Vol.XIX, pp.416-425.
2 Vol.II, pp.111-114.
3 pp.45-73.
4 pp.53.
5 pp.98.
6 See his argument in para.68 on page 27.
7 pp.151 (double col.).
8 quarto, 55 pp.
9 pp.56.
10 pp.256-262.
11 pp.17-42.
12 Bd.XX, pp.221-231.

cording to Meinhof's method. A curious little pamphlet by H.E.Ntsanwisi on *How to Write Shitron'ga* was published about this time.

(c) <u>Tswa</u>: This is the most important dialect of the Northern section, spoken inland from Inhambane. For all the grammatical and lexicographical work, as indeed for most of the very considerable literary output, we are indebted to J.A. Persson. In 1917 he published from the Inhambane Mission Press his <u>Outlines of Sheetswa Grammar</u> (with practical exercises)[1]; the second (greatly enlarged) edition of this, <u>Outlines of Tswa Grammar</u>[2] (1932) is a very creditable survey of the grammar, and completed the 'trilogy' with the works of Junod on Ronga and Tonga. Persson's work is fairly up-to-date in treatment. In 1928 he published <u>An English-Tswa Dictionary</u>[3], a work of considerable extent and scholarship. A 'Tswa-English Dictionary' is still awaited.

(5) <u>Inhambane Group</u>.

For Chopi (or Lenge) and Tonga (giTonga) of this group, there is very little of importance published. In 1902 Bishop Smyth and John Matthews published <u>A Vocabulary with a Short Grammar of Xilenge</u>[4] In 1933 H.P. Junod published at Lisbon <u>Eléments de grammaire tchopi</u>[5], a very brief outline.

In 1931 N.J. van Warmelo contributed to the 'Z.E.S.'[6] his <u>Das Gitonga</u>, a phonological study on the Meinhof principles, with a short vocabulary.

[6a] SOUTH-CENTRAL ZONE

Position: Southern Rhodesia and Portuguese East Africa.

Characteristics:
(1) A bridging between the Central Zone and the South-eastern, with certain resemblances to the East-central.
(2) Three-tone system.
(3) Staccato type of pronunciation.
(4) Peculiar phonetic phenomena including implosives, affricates and 'whistling fricatives', with the features of velarization and vocalization.
(5) Monosyllabic noun prefixes with latent initial vowel.
(6) Possessive form of relative construction.

---

1 pp.88.
2 pp.209.
3 pp.249 (double col.).
4 Vocabulary, pp.47; Grammar, pp.44.
5 pp.43.
6 Vol.XXII, pp.16-46.

(7) Noun diminutives and augmentatives formed by prefix (as well as suffixal diminutives).
(8) Locative prefix system.
(9) Deficient verbs.
(10) Ideophones.

Classification of languages: This zone comprises the Shona group of languages divided into the following clusters:

(1) Western, with dials: Nyai, Nambzya, Rozi, Kalanga, Talahundra, Lilima (Humbe), Peri.
(2) Northern, with dials: Tavara, Shangwe, Goʋa, Budya, Korekore (including: Tande, Nyongwe, Pfungwe, Sipolilo, Urungwe).
(3) Zezuru (Central), with dials: Shawasha, Haraʋa, Goʋa, Nohwe, Hera, Njanja, Mbire, Nobvu, Cikwakwa, Zimba, Tsunga.
(4) Karanga (Southern), with dials: Duma, Jena, Mhari, Goʋera, Ngoʋa, Nyubi.
(5) Eastern, with dials: Hungwe, Teʋe, Manyika, (including: Unyama, Karombe, Bunji, Nyamuka, Domba, Nyatwe, Guta, Bvumba, Here, Jindwi, Boca).
(6) South-eastern, with dials: Ndau, Tonga, Garwe, Danda, Shanga.

Of these no grammatical or lexicographical work has been done upon the various types of Western or of Northern. I deal with the others in turn.

(i) Karanga: In 1893 M.E. Weale published Matabele and Makalaka Vocabularies;[1] the author used a very misleading orthography, and much of his Karanga is incorrect. In 1915 appeared Mrs. C.S. Louw's A Manual of the Chikaranga Language[2], with grammar, exercises, conversational sentences and vocabularies. This book was for long the best grammatical sketch of any of the Shona dialects. The Karanga vocabulary contained over 8,000 words. In 1926 Mrs. G. Murray produced a little English-Chikaranga Dictionary, being some 50 pages of excerpts from Mrs. Louw's larger book.

(ii) Zezuru: In 1893 A.M. Hartmann brought out An Outline of a Grammar of the Mashona Language[3], a pioneering piece of work but one which revealed the author's faulty ear, for he frequently confused g and k, ts and dz, etc. In the next year he published his English-Mashona Dictionary[4], 'with appendix of some phrases'. The vocabulary contained some 2,000 English words. In 1897 W.A. Elliott published his Dictionary of

1 pp.32.
2 pp.x + 397.
3 pp.69.
4 pp.vi + 78.

the Tebele and Shuna Languages[1], containing a grammatical outline and dictionaries intended to cover several of the dialects of Mashonaland. His work on 'Shuna' is very inaccurate; he did not even recognise the 'whistling fricatives'. In 1906 E. Biehler brought out the first edition of his English-Chiswina Dictionary with an Outline Chiswina Grammar[2]. A new and enlarged edition was published in 1913[3], and a further revision in 1927[4]. This was for long the only real book of reference to Zezuru. In 1931 'B.St.' published as a special supplement A Grammar of Central Karanga[5] by F. Marconnès. This was a work of considerable scholarship, containing a deep analysis and a wealth of illustrative material. But it was marred by the author's infatuation for the ultra-disjunctive method of word-division. He, however, carried this to its logical conclusion and was bold enough to divide noun-prefix and noun-stem into two different words. The prefix he called an 'article'. Mainly dealing with Zezuru, this work also contains references to Karanga and Manyika.

(iii) Manyika: The first Manyika analysis was made by Mrs. H.E. Springer in her Hand-Book of Chikaranga or the Language of Mashonaland[6] published in 1905. Though based on Manyika, this work contained many words of Zezuru. A brief grammatical introduction was followed by vocabularies, about 3,000 Shona words being included. From her introduction one gathers that Mrs. Springer had a remarkable grip of the language position in Mashonaland. In 1911 H. Buck published A Dictionary with Notes on the Grammar of the Mashona Language, commonly called Chiswina[7]. This contained a simple grammatical sketch and a vocabulary of about 4,500 Manyika words. A Vocabulary of Chimanhica[8] was contained in the Mozambique Government publication, 'Respostas ao Questionário Etnográfico' of 1928.

(iv) Ndau: Bleek had included an Ndau vocabulary under the name of 'Sofala' in his 'Languages of Mosambique' of 1856. In 1911 Daniel Jones wrote The Pronunciation and Orthography of the Chindau Language[9], a brief analysis conducted with a Native Ndau and the assistance of Dr. W.L. Thompson. Dr. Thompson contributed to 'Nada', in 1927, A Uniform Phonetic Alphabet for the Native Languages of Rhodesia[10], based on Ndau or its dialect Shanga. In 1915 the American Board Mission published Chindau-English and English-Chindau Vocabulary with Grammatical Notes[11].

---

1 pp.xl + 398.
2 pp.263 + 120.
3 pp.288, followed by a 'Mashona or Chiswina Vocabulary' of 155 pages.
4 pp.428.
5 pp.xv + 270.
6 pp.106.
7 pp.206.
8 pp.1–25 at the end of the book, and also certain grammatical notes on pp.113–22.
9 pp.16.
10 pp.10.
11 pp.139.

The work was due principally to G.A.Wilder, who had collected a vocabulary of over 1000 words as far back as 1888, J.P. Dysart, C.C. Fuller and A.J. Orner. It contains about 4,000 Ndau words. In the Ndau-English section the nouns are listed according to the initial letters of their prefixes. Italicized letters are used to indicate many of the sounds not provided for by the Roman alphabet. The Mozambique Government publication 'Respostas, etc.' includes a vocabulary of Ndau, and a short grammatical study in which the Sena and Ndau verb conjugations are compared. J.P. Dysart prepared a manuscript of Chindau Lessons[1], which is widely used by American Board missionaries in learning the language.

During 1929 C.M. Doke undertook a survey of all the Shona dialects, with a view to advising the Government of Southern Rhodesia on the subject of unification. A direct result of this survey was seen in three publications: (i) Occasional Paper, No.2, of the Dept. of Native Development, The Problem of Word-Division in Bantu, with special reference to the languages of Mashonaland[2], in which a strong plea was made for the adoption of conjunctive writing for the area. This was published in 1929. (ii) Report on the Unification of the Shona Dialects[3], presented to the Legislative Assembly in 1931. This report, after giving statistics of population and language distribution, presented an outline of Shona phonetics, followed by recommendations for unification of orthography, grammar and vocabulary under the name of 'Shona'. A fairly complete bibliography for the area was included, as well as comparative vocabularies, a language map and subsidiary distribution maps. (iii) A Comparative Study in Shona Phonetics[4], which was the scientific report presented to the Carnegie Corporation, who had in part financed the research. The phonetic analysis covered all the cluster fields and dealt with 37 dialectal types. This contained the first detailed study of the phenomena of 'Vocalization' and 'Velarization', and was illustrated with kymograph tracings and palatograms.

As a result of the 'unification' proposals two further books have so far been published. In 1932 B.H. Barnes brought out, in the new orthography, A Vocabulary of the Dialects of Mashonaland[5], a very valuable piece of work in which dialectal differences were carefully indicated. In 1935 appeared J. O'Neil's A Shona Grammar (Zezuru dialect)[6]. Though this was in the new orthography and sponsored by the Committee on Unification, it is disappointing, as O'Neil used the new orthography against his own inclinations, and employed old methods of approach, while a certain amount of editing and the inclusion of Karanga and Manyika variants were done by B.H. Barnes. There is still need for a good unified Shona grammar.

---

1 97 typed quarto pages.
2 pp.22.
3 pp.156, with numerous folders.
4 pp.viii + 298.
5 pp.ix + 214.
6 pp.vi + 216.

[7] WESTERN ZONE

Position: West Coast of Africa south of Benguella to Mandated Territory of South-west Africa, and including central and southern Angola.

Characteristics:
(1) Use of a particular initial vowel, e.g. 'o' in Herero.
(2) Distinctive type of absolute pronoun.
(3) Use of copulative verb.

Classification of languages:
(1) Mbundu (uMbundu).
(2) Ambo group: Ndonga, Kwanyama.
(3) Herero.
(4) Nyaneka group: including Humbe, Mwila, etc.
(5) Yeye or Yeei.

(1) Mbundu.

This language, uMbundu of the Bihé Highlands, must be clearly distinguished from kiMbundu or Ndongo, which belongs to the Congo zone. A certain amount of useful information about investigations into this language is to be culled from L.D. Turner's article Linguistic Research and African Survivals contributed to the 'Bulletin of the American Council of Learned Societies'[1]. As early as 1843 Ladilaus Magyar, Hungarian traveller and slave-trader, illustrated Mbundu or 'Nano' by short vocabularies in the 'Proceedings of the Royal Geographical Society' in 1843, and in his 'Reisen' published in 1859. Both the missionary Rath and W.H.I. Bleek compiled lists of 'Nano' words. Capello and Ivens published a vocabulary in their 'Travels' (1882), as did Serpa Pinto in his 'How I crossed Africa' (1881). H. Schuchardt wrote a few pages Ueber die Benguela-sprache in a Vienna journal in 1883. The first real details, however, were given by W.M. Stover in 1885 when he published his Observations upon the grammatical structure and use of the Umbundu or the language of the inhabitants of Bailundu and Bihe, and other countries of West Central Africa.[2] This was quite a small work. In the same year W.H. Sanders and W.E. Fay brought out their Vocabulary of the Umbundu language, comprising Umbundu-English and English-Umbundu[3]. Other missionaries also contributed to this collection of some 'three thousand words'. Later editions more than doubled the number of entries: I have a mission-printed

---

1 No.32, Sept.1941.
2 pp.viii + 83; L.D. Turner also refers to a dictionary by Stover, but I have no further information upon this; a further edition of the 'Grammatical Notes' was published in 1919.
3 pp.76.

1911 edition with over seven thousand Mbundu words[1]. These vocabularies are little more than 'word-lists'. In 1894 J. Pereira do Nascimento published as No.102 of the 'Sociedade de Geographia, Boletim.13° serie', his Grammatica do Umbundu[2], characterised by H.H.Johnston as 'excellent'; and in the same 'Boletim' in 1897 appeared Ernesto Le Comte's Methodo Pratico da Lingua Umbundu[3]. In 1918 Helen Stover published at Bailundo First Lessons in Umbundu[4]; and in 1930 Amandus Johnson his Mbundu-English-Portuguese Dictionary at Philadelphia.[5] Dr. Merlin W. Ennis is preparing considerable M.S. material upon the Mbundu language[6]. In 1933 H.F.Schatteburg produced a small 37-page Sprachschatz des Umbundu. In 1935 R.L.Wilson published his Dicionário Prático, Portugûes-Umbundo[7], containing nearly 5000 common words; and in 1937 the Catholic Mission at Bailundo issued L. Keiling's Elementos de Gramática Mbundo of 75 pages.

(2) Ambo Group.

(a) Ndonga: C.G.Büttner published a short Vocabulary and grammatical note in the 'Zeitschrift' of the German Geographical Society in 1881. R. N. Cust refers to a grammar of the language written by Theophilus Hahn in 1883.[8] An adequate dictionary of Ndonga was included in parallel by H. Brincker in his important Wörterbuch und Kurzgefasste Grammatik des Otji-Hérero of 1886, which will be fully discussed when dealing with Herero. A short practical exposition of the language was given by A. Seidel in 1892 in his Praktische Grammatiken der Hauptsprachen Deutsch-Südwestafrikas: I Nama, II Otyiherero, III Oshindonga. The Ndonga grammar and vocabularies occupy pp.127-180 of this little book, and constitute mere outlines. In a similar manner P.H. Brincker included three languages in his 1897 study, Vergleichende Grammatik des Otjiherero, Osikuanjama und Osindonga.[9] In the Ndonga and Kwanyama sections of this book there are many mistakes, the work being done before a full investigation of these languages. In 1908 A. Savola published at Helsinki the only grammar of a Bantu language in Finnish of which we have knowledge — Ošindongan Kielioppi[10]. This is a practical grammatical exposition of Ndonga for the use of the Finnish Mission in Ovamboland. Very little recent work has been done on Ndonga, but mention might be made of Panconcelli-Calzia's Untersuchungen über die stimmlosen Nasale im Ndonga, contributed to the 'Z.f.K.S.'[11]

---

1 pp.648.
2 pp.105.
3 Of which I have no further information.
4 pp.106.
5 I have not seen this book, and further details are needed.
6 He is working out a detailed grammatical analysis.
7 pp.158.
8 I have not seen either of these items.
9 For details, see under Herero.
10 pp.vi, 134.
11 1917; Vol.VI, pp.257-263.

(b) Kwanyama: The traveller James Chapman included in his 'Travels in the Interior of South Africa', 1868, as an appendix to the second volume 'Notes on the Damara Language'. This contained vocabularies of 'Damara' (Herero), 'Ovambo' (Kwanyama) and 'Vanano' (Mbundu). Under the name of 'Humba' Capello and Ivens illustrated short vocabularies of Kwanyama in their 'Travels to the Territories of Yacca' (1882). In 1891 Brincker published his Lehrbuch des Oshikuanjama, which has a special value in the comparative study of Bantu languages. The book is in two parts, the first of which (pp. 1–118) is a grammatical exposition of Kwanyama with parallel treatment of Ndonga and Herero. The classification is 'old style' in which prepositions, etc. are recognised. The second part (pp.1–136) is a 'Wörterbuch des Oshikuanjama' with comparative entries for Ndonga and Herero, each of the three languages being indicated by a different style of type. Brincker also included a study of Kwanyama in his 'Vergleichende Grammatik' of 1897, already referred to. In 1910 H. Tönjes published two volumes in the series 'Lehrb. S.O.S. (Berlin)'[1], his Lehrbuch der Ovambo-sprache, Osikuanjama[2], and his Wörterbuch der Ovambo-sprache, Osikuanjama-Deutsch[3]. The former contained a fair phonological outline, a systematic grammatical study with exercises, considerable syntactical details, some pages of phrases and short vocabularies — altogether a very useful manual. The dictionary is a painstaking piece of work with considerable detailed information.

(3) Herero.

This is the chief language of the Western Zone, and considerable literary and other linguistic work has been done in it, mainly by German workers. Herero is spoken in the Mandated territory of South-west Africa. As early as 1857 C.H. Hahn had produced his Grundzüge einer Grammatik des Herero nebst einem Wörterbuche, detailed reference to which has already been made[4]. The next worker to claim our notice is F.W. Kolbe. Kolbe had commenced missionary work in this field in 1848, and in 1868 published a seven-page pamphlet, A Brief statement of the discovery of the laws of the vowels in Herero... bearing upon the origin and unity of language; and in 1869 a slightly larger pamphlet, entitled The Vowels; their primeval laws and bearing upon the formation of roots in Herero.[5] This was later (in 1888) further elaborated in his book, A Language study Based on Bantu, in which much Herero material is cited. In this work, however, Kolbe allowed his imagination to run away with his judgment, and it is a relief to turn from this sort of thing to his really sound piece of work, An English-Herero Dictionary[6], which had appeared in 1883. In this most useful book, Kolbe refers to certain sources: Hahn's 'Wörter-

---

1 Vols. XXIV and XXV.
2 pp.xii + 235.
3 pp. x + 271.
4 See 'Bantu Pioneers' pp.235–6.
5 pp.ii, 32.
6 pp.lv + 570 (double col.)

buch'; a manuscript Herero-German Dictionary by J. Rath, a copy of which is preserved in the Grey Library, Cape Town; a Herero-English Vocabulary appended by H. Brincker to his Herero Reading-book. This was a very full treatment, and was preceded by some 40 pages of grammatical outline.

In 1879 H. Brincker published a little 'second' reader entitled <u>Omahonge ookuleza Otyiherero</u>[1], to which he added a very considerable 'Vocabulary for translating this reading book into English', in which numerous grammatical notes are included. In 1886 Brincker published his well-known comparative lexical study of Herero — his <u>Wörterbuch und Kurzgefasste Grammatik des Otji-Herero</u>[2]. This is a fairly complete and thoroughly reliable dictionary, in which the Ndonga equivalents are added in italics. It is to be regretted that nouns are listed according to the forms of their prefixes and not under stems. Following the main body of the dictionary are a number of Herero Folk-tales with German interlinear translation. The thirty-one pages of grammar give a concise comparison of Herero and Ndonga ('Otj-ambo'), while some valuable grammatical tables are appended. A short grammar and vocabularies of Herero were included on pages 59-126 of A. Seidel's <u>Praktische Grammatiken der Hauptsprachen Deutsch-Südwestafrikas: I Nama, II Otyiherero, III Oshindonga</u>, which was printed in 1892. This was a concise work but contained many mistakes. In 1897 Brincker produced his <u>Vergleichende Grammatik des Otjiherero, Osikuanjama und Osindonga</u>[3].

In 1897 Brincker contributed to the 'Z.A.O.S.'[4] an article <u>Die Bedeutung der Nominalpräformative etc. von sechs Dialekten der Lingua Bantu</u>, dealing with Herero, Ndonga, Kwanyama, Mbundu, 'Kafir-Sulu' and Nyanja. In the same year appeared his <u>Deutscher Wortführer für die Bantu-dialekte in Südwest-Afrika</u>, a work characterised as good but not always reliable[5]. 1897 also saw the publication of G. Viehe's <u>Grammatik des Otjiherero nebst Wörterbuch</u>[6], by far the most complete and reliable work to date. Due space is given to syntax; phrases are added, and a vocabulary. In the same year, too, C.G. Büttner contributed a 40-page phrase book to the 'Z.A.S.'[7] entitled <u>Sprachführer für Reisende in Damaraland</u>. In 1899 C. Meinhof included in his 'Lautlehre' a chapter[8] on the phonology of Herero, treated on his principles of reference to the hypothetical Ur-Bantu forms. This chapter was omitted from the later English translation of the book. In

---

1 Reader pp.1-78, Vocabulary pp.79-218. No author's name is published, but an inscribed copy presented to Theophilus Hahn shews it to be Brincker.
2 pp.viii, 351, 31 and 7 tab.
3 I have not seen a copy of this.
4 Jahrg. III, pp.318-331.
5 I have not seen a copy.
6 pp.xii, 140.
7 I, pp.252-294.
8 Ch. VI, pp.113-141 (of the 2nd ed. 1910).

1909 Meinhof published a little study book for beginners, Die Sprache der Herero in Deutsch-Südwestafrika[1], as Vol.I of the series 'Deutsche Kolonialsprachen'. J. Irle was the author in 1917 of a Deutsch-Herero Wörterbuch[2], which contains a rich store of words, suitable for gaining a first knowledge of the language, but is far too uncritical.

(4) Nyaneka group:

Of the many dialects comprising this group very little is known. Nyaneka, the speech of the Huila Highlands in Central Angola, is illustrated by a Diccionario Portuguez-Olunyaneka[3] prepared by the missionaries of the Congregation of the Holy Spirit and Sacred Heart of Mary, and published in 1896, and by A.M. Lang's Ensaios de Grammatica Nyaneka of 1906.

Regarding Humbe, it seems that only a manuscript vocabulary is in existence.

(5) Yeye (Yeei) or Kuba, spoken in the Northern Kalahari area, northwards from Maun, was exemplified in short vocabularies by David Livingstone, C. J. Andersson and Passarge. A recent publication, Notes on the Noun Classes of some Bantu Languages of Ngamiland[4], by I. Schapera and D.F. van der Merwe, gives considerable grammatical information on this language.

[7a] WEST-CENTRAL ZONE

Position: Eastern Angola and North-western Rhodesia.

Characteristics:

(1) A buffer type between the Western zone and the Central zone with features of the Congo zone.
(2) An extreme type of vowel assimilation, in which the final vowel of the verb often assimilates with the stem vowel.
(3) A striking sub-division of the noun classes into animate and inanimate.

Classification:

(1) Lwena or Luvale, dial. Chokwe.
(2) Luchazi, Lwimbi; Mbunda, Nkangala.
(3) Lunda (Ndembo).
(4) Soli.

(1) Lwena, also called Luvale, is spoken on the upper reaches of the

---

1 pp.viii, 114.
2 pp.455 (double col.).
3 I have not seen either of these publications.
4 1942, mimeographed foolscap, pp.103.

Zambesi River and to the westward into Angola. Chokwe seems to be one of the principal dialectal forms. Apart from an early Livingstone vocabulary, the earliest analysis of this language is a short note in 1912 entitled Luena by W.A. Crabtree in the 'J.A.S.'[2]. This contained second-hand information and gave little detail. Burssens refers to a Petit Dictionnaire français-lwena, lwena-français, by G.Vettor, which I have not seen. In 1922 D.T. Hume produced his Lwena Grammar for Beginners, which was roneod, not printed. This comprised some 57 small foolscap pages, covering elementary grammatical notes, exercises and a key. The best exposition appeared in 1941, A.E. Horton's A Grammar of the Lwena Language.[3]

For Chokwe Burssens refers to a multi-copied English-Chokwe Vocabulary, Chokwe-English Vocabulary, and Chokwe Grammar Notes, issued from Luma, Kasayi. This evidently refers to M.B. MacJannet's Chokwe Grammar Lessons (quarto cyclostyled) of which I have a copy of the first 32 pages. T. Louttit published in Chicago in 1916 a Chokwe Grammar.[4] A. Delille contributed a short Inleiding tot de Chichoksche Spraakleer to the journal 'Congo'[5] in 1935.

(2) Luchazi, Mbunda, etc.:

There is some information regarding the languages of this group in certain vocabularies, e.g. Capello and Ivens' 'Kaluiana' vocabulary in their 'Journey to the Territories of Yacca' (1882), and A.W. Thomas' comparative vocabulary of Sikololo-Silui-Simbunda of 1916. MS. vocabularies of Luchazi are extant. L. Homburger dealt with Kwambi and Ilundu in her comparative study of the 'South-west group of Bantu Languages'[6]. C.M.N. White contributes information on certain of these languages, Some Comparative Notes on the Noun Prefixes of the West-central zone of Bantu Languages,[7] in which he deals with Lunda, Chokwe, Lwena, Luchazi and Lwimbi.

(3) Lunda: This is known as Ndembo or Lunda of Kalunda, and must be distinguished from Luunda of the Central zone. It is spoken to the southwest of the Luba region, on the eastern side of the Upper Kasai, mostly in Belgian Congo, but reaching into Angola and into Northern Rhodesia at the headwaters of the Kabompo River.

Vocabularies of the language were published as early as 1882 by Capello and Ivens, and by Héli Chatelain in 1894 in his 'Bantu Notes and Vocabularies'[8]. In 1889 H. de Carvalho published at Lisbon his Methodo

---

1 In the Grey Library, Cape Town.
2 Vol.XI, pp.394-400.
3 pp.85.
4 pp.47.
5 Vol.XVI, pp.366-374.
6 See Tome III, Fascicule 1,'Linguistique de Angola et Rhodesia', Mission Rohan-Chabot, 1925.
7 'African Studies', Vol.III, No.4, 1944.
8 'Journal of the American Geographical Society', No.II.

pratico para fallar a Lingua da Lunda.[1] Dr. Walter Fisher furnished me in 1919 with a manuscript vocabulary 'English-Lunda' and 'Lunda-English'; while later his son Singleton Fisher produced grammatical notes and exercises on the language (untitled) in four 'books', the first three (totalling 90 pages) being mission printed, and the fourth a roneod quarto of 42 pages. In 1943 C.M.N. White produced a small Lunda-English Vocabulary[2], dealing with the language around Balovale in Northern Rhodesia. Mrs. Singleton Fisher has in the press a Grammar of the language and is engaged on dictionary work.

(4.) Soli, spoken east of Lusaka in Northern Rhodesia, has many features common with the surrounding Central Bantu languages, but shews a western origin. For information upon this language we are indebted to two publications of B.I.C. van Eeden: The Phonology of Soli, contributed to the 'Z.E.S.'[3] in 1936, a study on the Meinhof principles, and The Grammar of Soli, an outline contributed to the 'Annals of the University of Stellenbosch'[4] in the same year.

---

1 1889, pp.64; de Carvalho also published in two volumes, Vocabularios dos dialectos dos povos do occidente de região tropico-austral da Africa, etc.
2 pp.48.
3 Vol.XXVI, No.4, pp.241-271.
4 Vol.XIV, Sectn. B, No.1, pp.1-51.

INDEX

[Principally of Languages (underlined) and Authors].

	Page		Page
Achten, L.	33	Bemba	37–38
Adams, H.M.	7	Bembe, dial. of Kongo	21
Africa Inland Mission		Bena	53
(Language Committee)	15	Benga	5–6
Aloys —	30	Bennie, J.	83
Ambo Group	102–103	Bennie, W.G.	84, 85, 86
Ambrosius, P.	77	Bentley, Mrs. H.M.	20
American Board Mission	99	Bentley, W.H.	17, 18–19
Amu, see Lamu		Berthoud, P.	95, 96
Anderson, G.N.	46	Best, J.	9
Anderson, V.A.	32	Beste —	87
Anderson, W.G.	70	Beyer, G.	88
Andersson, C.J.	105	Biehler, E.	99
Appleyard, J.W.	83	Binns, H.K.	55
Arabic Influence on Swahili	61, 62	Bira	30
Arabic Script in		Birkeli, E.	38, 39
Swahili	56, 57–58, 60	Bisa	39
Armstrong, Miss L.	15	Bishop, H.L.	95–96
Archbell, J.	92	Bithrey, W.B.	69
Ashton, Mrs. E.O.	59, 60	Biton, A.	9
Asu, dial. of Pare	48	Bittremieux, L.	22
Atangana, K.	8	Blackledge, G.R.	12
Augustiny, J.	45	Bleek, W.H.I.	3, 54, 65, 67, 70,
Aushi	38		71, 72, 95, 99, 101
		Bonatz, J.A.	83
Baca	87	Bondei	50
Bachmann, F.	87	Boone, O.	25
Badoux, Ch.	36	Bourquin, W.	86, 87
Bain, J.A.	66	Boyce, W.B.	83
Bangala, see Ngala		Brincker, H.	102, 103, 104
Bangi	29–30	Brinton, T.B.	36
"Bantu Botatwe",		Broomfield, G.W.	59, 64
see Tonga (ciTonga)		Brown, J.	88, 92
Barfield, J.	18	Brown, J.T.	92
Barlow, A.R.	14	Bruens, A.	5
Barnes, B.H.	37, 68, 100	Brusciotto, H.	17, 18
Basa	5	Brutel, E.	63
Bates, G.L.	9	Brutzer, E.	15
"Batoka", see Tonga (ciTonga)		Bryant, A.T.	75–76, 78
Baumann, O.	3	Bryant, J.C.	74
Bazett, M.	58	Bua	30
Beach, D.M.	86	Bube	3
Beech, M.W.H.	57	Buck, H.	99
Beecher, G.S.B.	15	Bud-M'Belle, I.	86
Beecher, L.J.	15	Bufe —	4

Buja, dial. of Ngala 29
Bulley, Miss. M.W. 69
Bulu 7, 9
Burssens, A. 20, 32, 35, 38n, 106
Burt, F. 57
Bushnell, J. 7
Bushongo, see Kuba
Butaye, R. 19
Büttner, C.G. 15, 34, 60, 102, 104
Bwale, see Bua
Bwende, dial. of Kongo 19

Cabral, A.A.P. 63, 70, 72, 73, 95
Caldwell, R. 68
Callaway, H. 77, 81n
Calloc'h, J. 30
Cambier, Fr. 19, 27
Cannecattim, B.M. de 18, 22
Capello, H.C. de B. 101, 103, 106
Capus, A. 44, 45
Carrie, Mgr. 21n
Carrington, J.F. 24
Casalis, A. 91
Casalis, E. 65, 89, 90, 92
Casset, A. 40
Central Orthography Committee 81
Chaga 48
Chapman, J. 103
Characteristics of Zones 2, 9, 16-17, 31, 42-43, 55, 65, 73, 97, 101, 105
Chatelain, C.W. 96
Chatelain, H. 23-24, 106
Chawner, C.A. 96
Chewa, dial. of Nyanja 67
Chikunda 70
"Chinyanja", see Nyanja
Chokwe, dial. of Lwena 106
Chopi 97
Christaller, T. 3
"Chuana," see Tswana
Chwabo 71n, 72, 73
Clark, G.J. 52
Clarke, J. 3
Clarke, J.A. 33
Classification:
    of Bantu Languages 1, 2
    of South-central zone 98
    of South-eastern zone 74

Clusters, of languages 1
Colenso, J.W. 74
Collard, H.J. 38
Colle, P. 64
Colyer, S. 93
Composition, study of 13
Congregation du St. Esprit et
    du St. Coeur 62, 105
Cordell, O.T. 52
Cork, Miss 25
Courboin, A. 28
Courtois, V.J. 70, 72
Crabtree, W.A. 12, 106
Craven, H. 18
Crawshaw, C.J. 84
Crisp, W. 92
Cust, R.N. 7, 102

da Cunha, A. 73
da Cunha, J. d'A. 23n, 53
Dahin, Fr. 9
Dahl, E. 44
Dahle, M. 77
Dahl's Law 14
Dale, A.M. 41n
Dale, G. 50
"Damara", see Herero
da Matta, J.D.C. 24
Daull, Fr. 62
Davidson, J. 25
Davies, D.C. 28
Davis, M.B. 10
Davis, W.J. 83
de Beerst, G. 38
de Boeck, E. 19, 27, 28
de Calonne-Beaufaict, A. 30
de Carvalho, H. 106, 107n
de Clercq, A. 22, 32, 33, 34, 35, 36
de Clercq, L. 21, 22
de Couto, A. 22
Deed, Miss F.I. 48
de Gama, F.J. 94
de Gregorio, G. 63, 71
de Hailes, Miss L.M. 25
de Jager, C.F. 91
de Jesus, S. 23
de Jonghe, E. 36
Delaunay, Fr. 63
Delille, A. 106

Delius, S.	62	Ewald —	47
Delorme, Fr.	7	Ewondo, dial. of Yaunde	9
Delplace, Fr.	19	Eyles, F.	78
Dempwolff, O.	45, 46, 51, 52		
Denoit, C.	11	Fang	7–8
Denolf, Fr.	27	Farinha, A.L.	95
Desmaroux, Fr.	72, 73	Fay, W.E.	101
de Souza e Oliveira, S.	23	Faye, C.	76n, 79
Dialectal study, in Swahili	58, 63	Faye, C.U.	79
Dialects	1	Fell, J.R.	40
Dias, P.	22	"Fernandian", see Bube	
Dieterlen, H.	91	Ferreira, Mrs.	69
Digo	47, 48	Finnish work	102
Dinkelacker, E.	4	Fiote, see (ka)Kongo	
Döhne, J.L.	74, 83	Fipa	40
Doke, C.M.	37, 38–39, 42, 74n, 79, 80, 86, 90, 100	Fisher, Mrs. S.	107
		Fisher, S.	107
Domet, S.	60	Fisher, W.	107
do Nascimento, J.P.	102	Fokken, H.A.	48
Dorsch, H.	5	Ford, W.H.	24
do Sacramento, J.V.	72	Forfeitt, W.	25
Drum-language	9	Fox-Pitt, T.S.L.	37
Duala	3–5, 6	Francina, M.A. de C.	23
Dufay, Fr.	14	Franz, G.H.	88
Duma	9	Frédoux, J.	92
Dupeyron, P.	71, 73	Froberville —	54
Duruma	47	Fuller, C.C.	100
Duta, H.W.	13		
Dutra —	23	Galaganza, dial. of Nyamwezi	44
Dutrieux, Fr.	62	Galwa	6, 7
Dysart, J.P.	100	Ganda	11–13
Dzing, dial. of Bangi	30	Ganga, speech of Swahili medicine men	58
Eddie, J.B.	25	Gaskin, E.A.L.	4
Edmiston, A.B.	27	Gautier, J.M.	6
Edwards, W.H.	29	Gérard, Fr.	30
Eiselen, W.	89, 96	Gerstner, J.	76
Eldred —	26	Gevrey —	65
Elge, C.	28	Gibbs, S.	75
Elliot, W.	65	Gikuyu	14–15
Elliott, W.A.	82, 98	Gilliard, L.	26
Elmslie, W.L.	66, 82	Gindo	51
Elphinstone, H.	59	Giryama	47, 48
Endemann, Ch.	94	Gishu	10
Endemann, K.	66, 87, 90	Gisu, see Gishu	
Endemann, T.M.H.	88, 89, 94	Gleiss, F.	49, 50
Engelbrecht, J.A.	80, 87	Gluckman, M.	93
Ennis, M.W.	102	Godfrey, R.	85, 86

Gogo	50, 52, 60	Hildebrandt, J.M.	65
Good, R.A.	9	Hinde, Mrs. H.	15
Goodall, E.B.H.	37	Hofmann, J.	15
Gorju, J.	13	Hollis, A.C.	57, 65
Graffin, Mgr.	9	Homburger, L.	106
Grant, E.W.	79	Hopgood, C.R.	41
Greenway, P.J.	58	Hörner, M.E.	49
Griffin, A.W.	40	Horton, A.E.	106
Groups, of languages	1	Hottentot influence on Xhosa	86
Grout, L.	74, 81	Hulstaert, G.	26
Guillain, —	65	Humba, see Kwanyama	
Guillerme, L.	37	Humbe, dial. of Nyaneka	105
Guilmin, M.	25	Hume, D.T.	106
Guiness, H.G.	17–18	Hunter, W.	83
Gujerati book on Swahili	63	Hurel, E.	11, 14
Guthrie, M.	28–29	Hynde, R.S.	71
Gwamba, dial. of Tonga (Shangana)	96	Ifumu, dial. of Teke	30
Gweno, dial. of Pare	48	Ikoma	45
		Ila	40, 41
Ha	14	Illaire, W. v S-P.	60, 62
Haarpaintner, M.	8	Ilundu, dial. of Luchazi	106
Haddon, E.B.	59	Ingram, W.H.	58
Hadimu, dial. of Swahili	58	Inkongo, see Luna-Inkongo	
Häfliger, J.	54	Inter-Territorial Language (Swahili)	
Hahn, C.H.	103	Committee to the East African	
Hahn, T.	102, 104n	Dependencies	59
Hale —	23, 54, 71	Inhambane Group	97
Hallowes, D.P.	87	Iramba	46
Handekyn, E.	27	Irangi	50, 52
Harries, L.	54	Irle, J.	105
Hartmann, A.M.	98	Isubu	5
Hattersley, C.W.	13	Italian Mission in East Africa	14
Heepe, M.	8, 65	Itio, dial. of Teke	30
Hehe	52	Ittameier, E.	46
Hellier, A.B.	56, 57n	Ittmann, J.	4
Hemba, see Luba-Hemba		Itumba, dial. of Sagara	51
Hemery, A.	14, 47	Ivens, R.	101, 103, 106
Henderson, J.E.	14		
Hendle, P.J.	52	Jacottet, E.	42, 87, 89, 90, 91, 92
Henga, dial. of Tumbuka	66	Jalla, A.	93
Henry, G.	67	Jankie, H.E.	90
Hensey, A.F.	26	Jannsens, A.	32
Herbert, T.	65	Jaques, A.A.	94n
Herero	102, 103–105	J.D.	37
Herrmann, C.	11, 45	Jenniges, E.	33
Heso, see So		Jenniges, J.M.	33
Hetherwick, A.	68–69, 71, 72	Jensen, H.	62

Jita	45	Kondoa, dial. of Sagara	51
Johnson, A.	102	Kongo	16, 17–22, 36
Johnson, F.	46, 54, 57, 64	– (kaKongo)	21–22
Johnston, H.H.	3, 10, 12, 23, 25,	– (kiKongo)	17–21
37, 38, 39, 43, 44n, 47, 48, 51, 53,		– (kishiKongo)	17, 19, 20
54, 66, 67, 70, 72, 87, 95, 102		"Kongo-Overzee"	35
Jones, Daniel	93, 99	Konjo	10
Jones, D.P.	38	Konongo, dial. of Nyamwezi	44
Jordan, A.C.	87	Kotz, E.	48
Juanola, J.	3	Krapf, L.	15, 46, 47, 55–56, 60,
Junod, H.A.	95, 96, 97		67, 71
Junod, H.P.	97	Kriel, T.J.	88
		Kropf, A.	85
"Kaffir", "Kafir", see Xhosa		Krüger, F.	94
Kaguru	50, 51	Kruger, F.H.	89, 90, 91n, 93
"Kalaka", see Karanga		Krumm, B.	53, 59n, 62
Kalanga	98	Kuba	27
Kamanga, dial. of Tumbuka	66	Kuba (Ngamiland), see Yeye	
Kamba	15	Kumu-Bira, see Bira	
Kami	50, 51	Kuria	45–46
Kanyoka	36	Küsters, M.	58, 60
Kaonde	32, 34	Kwambi, dial. of Luchazi	106
Karanga	98, 99, 100	Kwanyama	102, 103, 104
Karlman, E.	21	Kwaya	45
Keiling, L.	102	Kwena, dial. of Tswana	92
Kela	27	Kwenyi, dial. of Sagara	51
Kele (diKele)	9	Kwiri	5
Kele (loKele)	9, 24		
Kempe, A.R.	80		
Kerewe	10–11	Lacustrine Group	45–46
Kersten, O.	65	Lala	38, 39
Kete	33	Laman, K.E.	16n, 17, 20–21, 30
Kgalagadi, dial. of Tswana	92	Lamba	38–39
Kikuyu, see Gikuyu		Lammond, W.	37
Kilimanjaro Group	48	Lamu, dial. of Swahili	57, 58
Kinga	54–55	Lang, A.M.	105
Kingon, T.R.L.	85	LangHeinrich, F.	49
Kisbey, W.H.	50	Largeau, V.	7
Kitchen-Kafir	28, 82–83	Last, J.T.	15, 37, 39, 44, 45, 50,
Kitchen-Swahili	64		51, 52, 53, 65, 72
Klamroth, M.	54	Laws, R.	68
Klingenheben-v. Tiling, M.	62	Le Berre, Mgr.	6, 7
Koelle, S. 17, 21, 30, 36n, 67, 71,		Le Comte, E.	102
	72	Leisegang, H.K.	80
Koko	5	Lejeune, L.	7
Kolbe, F.W.	103	Lenge, see Chopi	
Kololo	87, 93	Lenje, see Mukuni	
Komoro	58, 65	Lepsius' System	87
Konde, see Nkonde		Lestrade, G.P.	89, 91, 93

Le Veux, H.	11, 12	Maes, J.	25, 33
Liesenborghs, O.	63	Maeyens, L.	30
Lilani, A.S.	63	Magyar, L.	101
Lindblom, G.	15	Makei, dial. of Fang	7
Livingstone, D.	23, 40, 42, 54, 105	Makonde	53, 72
Livinhac, L.	11–12	Makua	71, 72–73
Lolo, see Mongo		Mambwe, dial. of Bemba	37, 38
Lomwe, dial. of Makua	71, 72	Mang'anja, dial. of Nyanja	67–68
Longland, F.	27	Mangoaela, Z.D.	90
Lorenz, A.	54	Manyika	76n, 99, 100
Louttit, T.	106	Maples, C.	54, 71, 72
Louw, Mrs. C.S.	98	Maravi, see Peta	
Lovedu, dial. of Northern Sotho	89	Marconnes, F.	99
Loze, P.	95, 96	Marichelle, C.	22
Lozi	93	Marker, J.H.	28
Luba	32–36, 106	Marole, L.T.	94
— "Luba-commune"	32, 34	Martrou, L.	7
— Luba-Hemba	32, 33	Masaba, see Gishu	
— Luba-Lulua	32–33	Mate, P.	75
— Luba-Sanga	32, 33–34	Matengo	54
Luchazi	106	Mathabathe, T.P.	88
Lulua, see Luba-Lulua		Mathieu, Ch.	9
Luna-Inkongo	32, 34	Matthews, J.	97
Lunda	36, 106–107	Matumbi	53
Lundu	5	Maugham, R.C.F.	73
Lundwe, dial. of Ila	42	Maviha	53, 54
Lungu, dial. of Bemba	38	Mawanda, see Ndonde	
Luunda	36, 106	Mayr, F.	77
Luvale, see Lwena		Mbamba	24
Lux, Herr,	23	Mbangala	24
Luyi	42	Mbata, A.H.S.	80
Lwena	105–106	Mbunda	106
Lwimbi	106	Mbundu (kiMbundu) see Ndongo	
		Mbundu (uMbundu)	22, 101–102, 103, 104
Maass —	51		
Mabale	29	Mbwabe	72
Mabille, A.	88, 89, 91	Mbwera	36
MacBeath, A.G.W.	29	McElroy, W.F.	32
MacJannet, M.B.	106	McGregor, A.W.	14
MacKenzie, D.R.	66	McKee, G.T.	32
MacKenzie, Mrs.	26n	McKinnon, A.C.	33
MacKenzie, T.C.	28	McKittrick, F.T.	25
Mackey, J.L.	5	McKittrick, J.	25
Macvicar, N.	85	McLaren, J.	83–84, 85, 86
Madan, A.C.	37, 38, 39, 42, 55n, 56, 57, 61, 64, 69, 85	Mdhladhla, G.C.S.	80
		Medicine men, Speech of, in Swahili	58
Maddox, H.E.	10		
Madiba, M.J.S.	89, 90	Medo, dial. of Makua	72

Meinhof, C.	3, 4, 5, 8, 20, 30, 44, 45, 46, 47, 48, 49, 50, 51, 53, 54, 61, 66, 72, 73, 80, 86, 87, 88, 93, 97, 104–105
Melzian, H.J.	4
Ménard, F.	13
Merrick, J.	3
Mertens, J.	30
Meru, dial. of Chaga	48
Messi, P.	8
Meyer, E.	69
Mfengu	87
Mgao, dial. of Swahili	58
Missionaires de Scheut	28
Missionaries, American Baptist	26
— American, of Gabun	6
— Baptist, at Yakusu	24
— French Catholic, of Gabun	6
— of Congrégation du Saint-Esprit et du Saint-Coeur de Marie	6
Mission de Landana	21
Missions Salésiennes	38n
Mohl, A.	71
Moltedo, G.	63
Mongo	25–27
Moon, E.R.	26
Moreira, A.	70
Morrison, W.M.	27, 32
Moshi, dial. of Chaga	48
Mpondo, dial. of Xhosa	87
Mpongwe	6–7
Mrima, dial. of Swahili	58
Mudau, E.F.N.	94
Mukuni	40, 41, 42
Mundi, dial. of Swahili	58
"Muntu", see Yao	
Murray, Mrs. G.	98
Murray-Jardine, G.	58
Mvita, dial. of Swahili	55, 56, 57, 58
Mwali, dial. of Komoro	65
Mwamba, dial. of Nkonde	66
Mwera	54
Nagel, E.	84
Namwanga	40
"Nano", see Mbundu	
Nassau, R.H.	5, 7
Ndau	99–100

Ndeɓele, dial. of Zulu	74, 81–82
Ndeɓele (Transvaal), dial. of Zulu	74, 82
Ndembo, see Lunda	
Ndonde	54
Ndonga	102, 103, 104
Ndongo	22–24, 101
Ndumu	9
Nekes, H.	4, 8
New, E.	47
Newton, A.J.	84
Ngala	27–29, 36
— (baNgala)	27, 28
— (liNgala)	27–29
Ngazija, dial. of Komoro	51, 58, 65
Ngelima, dial. of Bua	30
Ngindo, dial. of Yao	72
Ngombe	25
Ngoni, dial. of Zulu	54, 74, 82
Ngovi, see Ngozi	
Ngozi, dial of Swahili	56, 58
Nguni Group	74–87
Nguru, dial. of Zigula	50
Nguruimi	45
Ngwana	36, 63
"Nika"	47–48
Nkonde	66
Nkosi	5
Nkoya	36
Nkunda, dial. of Sagara	51
Nkundu	25–26
Nkutshu, see Tetela	
Nkwifiya, dial. of Sagara	51
Noel, E.	38
Nsenga	69–70
Ntomba	26–27
Ntsanwisi, H.E.	97
Nyakyusa, see Nkonde	
Nyamwezi	43–45
Nyaneka Group	105
Nyanja	67–69, 104
Nyanyembe, dial. of Nyamwezi	44
Nyasa Group	66–67
Nyaturu	45
Nyoro	10
Nyungwe	70–71, 72
Nzwani, dial. of Komoro	65
O'Flaherty, P.	12
Omyene	7
O'Neil, J.	82, 100

O'Neill, H.E.	53, 54, 72	Rankin, D.J.	72
Orner, A.H.	100	Ratcliffe, B.J.	59
Orthography: Shona	100	Rath, J.	101, 104
— Tswana	93	Raum, J.	48
— Xhosa	86	Reallon, L.	5
— Zulu	78, 81	Rebmann, J.	47, 67
Otto, Br.	78	Reeb, A.	9
"Ovambo", see Kwanyama		Rehse, H.	11
Ovir, E.	61	Reichart, A.	58, 60
		"Rhodesian Ndebele", see Ndebele	
"Pahouin", see Fang		Riddel, A.	67
Paiva, R.	95	Robert, M.	7
Palmer, A.B.	29	Roberts, C.	75, 77, 83
Panconcelli-Calzia, G.	62, 102	Robertson, W.G.	37
Pangwa	54	Roehl, K.	14, 49, 59, 62
Pare	48	Roland, H.	34
Parr —	3	Rolong, dial. of Tswana	92
Passarge, S.	105	Ronga	95–96, 97
Passy, P.	96	"Rori", see Sango	
Pate, dial. of Swahili	57, 58	Rosenhuber, S.	5
Pedi, dial. of Northern Sotho	87–89	Rösler, O.	49
Peeraer, S.	35	"Rotse", see Luyi	
Pemba, dial. of Swahili	58	Rowling, F.	13, 47n
Pepo, dial. of Swahili	58	Rubben, E.	28
Perrin, J.	74	Rufiji Group	52
Persson, J.A.	97	Ruguru	51
Peta, dial. of Nyanja	67	Rundi	8, 13–14
Peters, W.	65	Ruskin, E.A.	25–26
Phuthi, dial. of Xhosa	87	Ruskin, L.	25–26
Pichon, Fr.	9	Russian work	81
Pilkington, G.L.	12	Rwanda	13–14
Pinheiro, A.S.	95		
Pinto, Serpa	101	Sacleux, Ch.	7, 63, 65
Plaatje, S.T.	93	"Sagalla", dial. of Taita	47
Planert, W.	8, 62	Sagara	51–52, 60
Pogoro	52–53	Saker, A.	3
Pokomo	46	Salt, H.	72
"Pondo", see Mpondo		Salvadó y Cos	6
Poto	24–25	Samain, A.	34
Presbyterian Mission	9	Samuelson, R.C.A.	75, 76, 79
Preston, J.M.	9	Sanders, W.H.	101
Price, E.W.	25	Sanderson, M.	69, 72
Price, T.	69	Sanga, see Luba-Sanga	
Prichard, J.C.	22n	Sango	53
Proyart, Abbé	21	Santu, dial. of Teke	30
Purvis, J.B.	10	Savola, A.	102
		Schapera, I.	92, 105
Quinot, H.	35	Schattenburg, H.F.	102
		Schebesta, F.P.	70
Raddatz, H.	52, 60	Schillebeeckx, I.	29
Ranger, A.S.B.	70	Schoeffer, Fr.	37

Schregel, W.	45	Soveral, A. de C.	72
Schreuder, H.P.S.	74, 77, 80	Spanish work	3, 7
Schrumf, C.	89, 92	Sparshott, T.H.	47
Schuchardt, H.	101	Spiss, C.	52, 54, 82
Schuler, E.	5	Springer, Mrs. H.E.	99
Schumacher, Fr.	14	Stanley, H.M.	11, 39, 50, 53
Schumann, C.	53, 66	Stapleton, W.H.	19, 24-25, 27, 29
Schürle, G.	5	Starr, F.	21, 56
Schwellnus, P.E.	88, 94	Stavem, O.	80
Schwellnus, T.	94	Steenberg, O.S.	77
Scott, D.C.	68	Steere, E.	44, 49, 50, 53, 56, 57, 65, 71
Scott, R.R.	58		
Seidel, A.	4, 20, 44, 45, 46n, 48, 49, 51, 52, 60, 61, 64, 102, 104	Stern, R.	44
		Stewart, J.	84
Selmer, E.W.	81	Steytler, J.G.	69
Sena	70-71, 72, 100	Stigand, C.M.	58
Senga, see Nsenga		Stirke, D.E.C.	42, 93
"Sesuto", see Sotho		Stover, Helen	102
Shambala	49-50	Stover, W.M.	101
Shanga, dial. of Ndau	99	Struck, B.	10, 40, 44n, 65
"Shangaan", see Tonga (Shangana)		Struyf, I.	20
Shangana-Tonga, see Tsonga		Stuart, J.	81n
Shaw, A.D.	15, 47, 56	Stuart, P.A.	78
Sheane, J.H.W.	37	Subiya	42
Shela, dial. of Swahili	58	Sudanic	5, 27
Shona	82, 98-100	Sukuma	44, 45
"Shuna", see Shona		Sumbwa	44, 45
Siha, dial. of Chaga	48	Sumerian	12, 79
Sillery, A.	45	Suter, F.	78
Simon, H.	71	Sutu	54
Sims, A.	24, 29, 30	Swahili	12, 36, 47, 51, 52, 55-64
Siu, dial. of Swahili	57, 58	— "Kitchen", "Up-country"	64
Skolaster, H.	5	Swan, C.A.	33
Slack, C.	56	Swarg, C.H.	5
Smith, E.W.	40, 41	Swazi	74, 87
Smith-Delacour, E.W.	95	Swedish work	19, 20, 21
Smyth, W.E.	97		
Sneguireff, I.L.	81	"Tabele", see Ndebele	
Snoxall, R.A.	10	Tabwa	38
Snyder, D.W.	33	Taita	47
So	24	Tanganyika Education Department	58
Soko, see So		Tanghe, J.	16n, 27n, 29
Soli	107	Tate, H.R.	15, 47
Solongo, dial. of Kongo	22	Taveta	47, 48n
Solwe, see Kondoa		Taylor, W.E.	47, 48, 56, 57, 58
Songe	32, 34	"Tebele", see Ndebele	
Sotho Group	87-93	Teke	30
— Northern	87-89	Terminology	64
— Southern	87, 89-92	Tetela	27

Thomas, A. W.	42, 93, 106	van Mol —	28
Thompson, W.L.	99	van Scheut —	35
"Thonga", see Tonga (Shangana)		van Warmelo, N.J.	80, 82, 91, 94, 96, 97
Tielemans, E.P.	64		
Tikulu	46, 57, 58, 64—65	Van Zyl, H.J.	88
Tikuu, see Tikulu		Velten, C.	44, 51, 52, 61
Tlaro, dial. of Tswana	92	Venda	93—94
Tlhaping, dial. of Tswana	92	Verbeken, A.	35
Tone	20, 24, 25, 26, 29, 30, 59, 80, 86, 93	Vermeersch, G.	35
		Verpoorten, —	26
Tonga (chiTonga of Nyasa)	66—67	Vettor, G.	106
Tonga (ciTonga)	40—41, 42	Victor, N.	58
Tonga (giTonga)	97	Viehe, G.	104
Tonga (Shangana)	96—97	Vili, dial. of Kongo	22
Tönjes, H.	103	Vinson, T.C.	32
Torday, E.	27	Visseq, A.	21—22
Toro	10	von Baudissin, —	61
Torre do Valle, E.	95	von Gravenreuth, F.F.	60
Torrend, J.	3, 40, 42, 65, 70, 71, 72, 73, 83	von Sowa, R.	53, 54
		Vumba, dial. of Swahili	58
Toulmond, L.	29		
"Transvaal Ndebele", see Ndebele (Transvaal)		Walker, A.	7
		Walther, K.	48
Trapp, O.O.	82	Wanger, W.	76, 78—79
Tsonga	94—97	Watkins, M.H.	67
Tswa	97	Watt, S.	15
Tswana	87, 92—93	Weale, M.E.	81, 98
Tucker, A.N.	60, 89, 91, 93	Welsh, G.H.	84, 86
Tugulu, dial. of Makua	72	Werner, A.	45, 49, 58, 72, 79
Tumbatu, dial. of Swahili	58	Werner, M.	58
Tumbuka	66	Werther, C.W.	44, 51, 52
Turner, L.D.	101	Westcott, W.H.	34
Twa, dial. of Mukuni	42	Westermann, D.	66
		Westlind, N.	19
Unguja, dial. of Swahili	55, 57, 58	Westlind, P.A.	21
Unification of Shona	100	White, C.M.N.	106, 107
Union of Bemba Language Committee	37	White, W.H.	25
		"White Fathers"	37
Ussel, A.R.	21n	Whitehead, J.	29
		Wiese, H.	80
van Acker, A.	38	Wilder, G.A.	100
van Bulck, G.	20	Wilson, C.E.	47
van der Burgt, J.M.M.	8, 13	Wilson, C.T.	11
Vandermeiren, J.	33	Wilson, J.L.	6
van der Merwe, D.F.	92, 105	Wilson, R.L.	102
van Eeden, B.I.C.	91, 107	Wolff, R.	54
van Ginneken, J.	71	Wolters, A.	11
van Hagen, G.T.	9	Womersley, H.	33
van Hove, Fr.	27	Woods, R.E.B.	34

Woodward, H.W.   47, 49, 50, 54, 73
Woodward, Miss. M.E.   68, **69**
Wookey, A.J.   92
Word-division   78n, 81, 100
Worms, A.   51
Wray, J.A.   47
Würtz, F.   46, 47, 64

Xhosa   74, 82, 83—87

Yalulema   24
Yanzi, see Bangi
Yao   71—72
Yaunde   5, 7, 8—9
Yeei, see Yeye
Yeye   105
Yombe, dial. of Kongo   21, 22
Young, T.C.   66

Zabala, A.O.   7
Zambesi Group   42
Zanake   45
Zaramo   50—51
Zezuru   98—99
Ziba   11
Ziervogel, D.   87
Zigula   50
Ziraha, dial. of Sagara   51
Zones, of languages   11
 — Central   30—42
 — Congo   16—30
 — East-central   65—73
 — Eastern   42—55
 — North-eastern   55—65
 — Northern   9—15
 — North-western   2—9
 — South-central   97—100
 — South-eastern   73—97
 — West-central   105—107
 — Western   101—105
Zulu   59, 74—83, 104

For Product Safety Concerns and Information please contact our EU representative GPSR@taylorandfrancis.com
Taylor & Francis Verlag GmbH, Kaufingerstraße 24, 80331 München, Germany